FIGHT BACK TO ETERNITY

Fight Back To Eternity

Patricia Chopping

The Creating Formula by Diamond Alpha Omega

© 2014 by Diamond Alpha Omega All rights reserved.

No part of this book may be reproduced in any written, electronic, recording, or photocopying without written permission of the publisher or author. The exception would be in the case of brief quotations embodied in the critical articles or reviews and pages where permission is specifically granted by the publisher or author.

Although every precaution has been taken to verify the accuracy of the information contained herein, the author and publisher assume no responsibility for any errors or omissions. No liability is assumed for damages that may result from the use of information contained within.

Publisher's Name - Diamond Alpha Omega

ISBN: 1507869347
ISBN 13: 9781507869345

TABLE OF CONTENTS

Dedication v
Preface vii
Prologue ix
Chapter 1 1
Chapter 2 3
Chapter 3 13
Chapter 4 15
Chapter 5 17
Chapter 6 19
Chapter 7 24
Chapter 8 27
Chapter 9 29
Chapter 10 32
Chapter 11 36
Chapter 12 40
Chapter 13 43
Chapter 14 45
Chapter 15 48

Chapter 16	54
Chapter 17	59
Chapter 18	62
Chapter 19	66
Chapter 20	69
Chapter 21	72
Chapter 22	75
Chapter 23	78
Chapter 24	81
Chapter 25	88
Chapter 26	93
Chapter 27	96
Chapter 28	104
Chapter 29	109
Chapter 30	123
Chapter 31	126
Chapter 32	129
Chapter 33	138
Chapter 34	140
Chapter 35	145
Chapter 36	152
Chapter 37	157
Chapter 38	171
Chapter 39	185
Chapter 40	190
Chapter 41	194
Chapter 42	197
Chapter 43	202
Chapter 44	210

DEDICATION

Dedicated to my dear husband, who encouraged me to write this book, whilst taking care of me after surgery. Also to my much loved son and daughter, who have helped me, on this incredible journey. With special thanks to my Spiritual Parents, who have always been there for me, on this journey known as life.

Whilst being a true account, where appropriate, the characters in this book, have been afforded Pseudonyms, for their personal anonymity. If the changed names, bear any resemblance to those living or dead, this is purely coincidental.

Also dedicated to the Planet Earth, in the hope that mankind, may learn to take better care of her and all those that dwell upon her.

PREFACE

Diamond is a World Renowned and highly respected Psychic Medium, who has received calls from all over Europe, in fact the Globe. Afghanistan, Iraq, China, Japan, Portugal, United States of America, India, Australia, Canada and New Zealand to name just a few, requesting readings and help, in many diverse ways. Her skills are without doubt or question and her clientele are from all walks of life. This Lady asks no questions but clearly answers all, getting straight to the point, as numerous people have so often attested to and is therefore, very highly respected because of this. Because Diamond is quietly spoken and eloquent, this belies her initial background. Her following can be forgiven, for perhaps believing that she was born with a silver spoon in her mouth, whilst nothing could be further from the truth. The reader will in fact, come to clearly appreciate that Diamond came from very humble beginnings and had to overcome her adverse family background and lack of early education, which was denied her from the outset. Her determination to rise above the many obstacles and mental traumas and illnesses, during her extraordinary childhood years and through her will to overcome these, through self education, to become the eloquent, highly respected person, she is today. Diamond herself, would be the very first to admit that the anomalous is true and the love, help and guidance, emanated from beyond the Veil.

I am aware that Diamond, is in the process, of writing another book, entitled Diamond's Psychic Diaries and I for one, eagerly await it's publication.

Saint

PROLOGUE

The veil has not yet closed and I am still seeking the meaning of life and aware that I am looking for light and knowledge

CHAPTER 1
MY QUEST FOR KNOWLEDGE AND THE REASON FOR INCARNATION

As I sit here in bed after foot surgery, following yet another reconstruction of my left foot, destined to be confined here for the next five weeks at the very least, my husband urges me to write this true story, which encapsulates life and those who look out for us all from beyond the veil. I believe that we incarnate through many life times, to gather information and to grow spiritually. Fight back to Eternity is my Spiritual quest to find out the truth and meaning of the various patterns of experience that link us all together. The paranormal that is mentioned in this book, started at an early age.

There are many of us earthly souls, who go through similar or identical patterns, regarding our various lifetime experiences. Those of us who have lost loved ones, be it adult or child and when this happens, we quite often have a Spiritual experience. Many of us may dismiss the contact with Spirits, as a figment of the imagination. Some talk about this with friends or family openly, thus discovering that they too, have experienced Spiritual contact. This book is based on my own Spiritual experiences, my Psychic, Clairvoyant, Healing and Exorcism abilities, using nothing more, than the light from God's energy, which we all have within us.

I have searched through various religions hoping to get the answers. Most have some element of Spiritual truths but there is always many questions left unanswered and we are then left to blind faith. I have found though, that when we are truly tuned into our Spirit Guides, Angels of God, especially in times of need, we get the answers. It would appear that in this particular lifetime my task was to discover, as many of the main poignant experiences as possible, that Spirit put me through, in order to have empathy, with those that Spirit wished to help. As my life opened up, my understanding and Spiritual knowledge grew. As you read this book many of you, will be able to relate to the various points and issues and when you get to the end of this book, you will find a very valid explanation, of the processes that come into force, which are and always have been there, for you cannot possibly destroy energy. So let me take you firstly by the hand of the child that I was then, leading you onward to the Medium I was destined to become.

CHAPTER 2
MY FIRST SPIRIT RECOLLECTION OF THIS LIFE ON EARTH BEGINS

I am a baby but I can think and reason in an adult way, for my consciousness still retains some memory, of a previous incarnation. Whilst I now occupy an infantile body, which I have yet to learn to have control over, thereby to speak, walk and learn.

My very first recollections of those who are beyond the veil began when I was sitting up in my pram, the year being 1948, for this was post war Britain. The pram was placed outside the air raid shelter, just a viewpoint from the kitchen window, of the ground floor flat, which I later found, was number 4 Rockfield house. Our mother approached us, breaking a piece of chocolate in two and gave half to me and half to my twin sister. I remember thinking, even at that early age, that if I ate mine first and then ate my sister's piece of chocolate, as she couldn't talk as yet, I would get away with it. So when my mother had left and gone back into the front door of the ground floor flat, I quickly ate my piece and then my sister Pam's also. My mother heard her cries of woe and protestations and came to see what was wrong and I was correct in thinking, my sister could not explain to her, exactly what I had done. However, later my Heavenly Parents appeared and chastised me, telling me that I was very naughty. I realized then, that I was an adult Spirit in an Earthly body, that could not as yet communicate, with those around me. Also I realized, that if ever I did anything wrong in life, I would never be able to get away with it. In some ways this was a good thing, I had learned a good and valuable lesson, with my sister being the one, who thought she could get away with anything and everything in life and invariably did.

At this point, I feel I should make it clear to the reader, that being an adult Spirit in an Earthly infantile body, made it possible for me to talk, with those beyond the veil and focus and comprehend things around me, in an adult manner, as opposed to that of the child, I in fact was.

My mother parked the large twin pram, which she had borrowed from a neighbor, outside the old bomb shelter. It was far enough from the ground floor flat, at 4 Rockfield House in Greenwich but close enough so that she could see it.

This was done on a daily basis and as time went by, I found myself placed in this pram on my own, more often than not, come rain or shine. My father later told me that I had contracted double pneumonia, whilst left out in the cold and rain. I was rescued by a neighbor and taken to St. Alfege's Hospital in Vanbrugh Hill, Greenwich and on arrival I was placed in an oxygen tent, to assist my breathing.

However I digress, the flats are those that are sited, opposite the Cutty Sark in Greenwich, South East London and at the time which was post war 1948, this was just a piece of grassland. Goats grazed there every day, and this area was in fact yet to become, the final resting place of the famous Cutty Sark.

A Mr. Wills owned this land, a very unkempt man, who always looked like he slept with his goats and surprisingly had an uncanny resemblance to them, due to his goatee beard. Often as I grew up, I could see Spirit children happily playing there, dancing around and patting the goats, who were totally and utterly oblivious to their presence. They were an immense source of happiness and contentment, whenever I looked at them. It later transpired that Mr Wills sold this land, for the princely sum, of £300.

My mother shunned me and had very little time for me whatsoever, whilst it was the complete opposite, regarding my twin sister. She was allowed to play, whilst I remained mainly in my cot, or the carriage pram outside the bomb shelter and I became to feel increasingly safer in this pram, than I did in the flat.

My mother was always screaming and shouting abuse at the top of her voice and this got worse when my father was around. On one occasion I recall, that she had cooked some greens, potato and sausage in the afternoon. It was a couple of hours or so, before my father was due back from work, leaving the plate above a pan of hot water, to keep it warm. Why had she made it so early I wondered? For she knew when my father finished work. I could see her anger increasing and when my father entered through the doorway, my mother had the hot plate of food in her gloved hand, the meal having dried to the plate. She then aimed the plate at my father, thankfully however, he moved to one side, with the plate narrowly missing him and hitting the front door, with the broken plate and it's contents, ending up all over the floor. I had so wanted to see my father and let him know that I had missed him, however he made a quick exit and did not return for a week. I was later to find out why my mother, hated both my father and I so much, for I heard words like, "If it wasn't for you and that horrible cuss of a kid of yours, things would be a lot easier around here." I couldn't at the time, understand why she hated my father so much, as he was a hard working coal man and part time blacksmith. Neither could I understand, why so much hatred, was vehemently directed towards me. The thing that I remember so vividly, from an early age and to this very day, was my mother's intense hatred of me. I so wanted her to hug me, as she did my twin sister, so why - oh why! not me?

My Heavenly Parents came to my rescue, as my mother had neither the time or the inclination to bother with me. "Put your hands on the wall" they said, "Pull yourself up, now steady yourself with your hand and face forward, now walk." This I did and thus I learned to walk.

As previously mentioned my father worked as a Coal man and part time Blacksmith, with his yard being in Deptford, just along from Barclay's Bank. He also had a Rag and Bone round at one time, for one of his many brothers. My aunts and uncles were numerous, as were my cousins, however for whatever reason, I rarely got to see them.

My father didn't come home much, for when he did there were always rows. My name was usually mentioned and that of a woman, who he was constantly accused of seeing.

My father was always cheerful, when he was with me and one day he brought his shire horse Queenie home, so that I could see her, much to the annoyance of my mother. Having just learned to walk, I toddled in and out of Queenie's legs. She just looked at me and didn't even budge at all, for I had formed a psychic link with her instantly. Queenie loved to see children, and Spirit assured me that she would never harm me.

My mother shouted at him, to get the horse back to the stables and not to bring it round to the flats again. "Take that horrible cuss of a kid with you too, and both of you get out of my sight," Heavenly Bliss, now I could get away from her, for a short while. As we left the grounds of the flat, whilst it was a bitterly cold and dismally dank day and I myself was cold, I didn't care in the least. Just being with my beloved father, that was all that mattered. I could see men going about their business, dressed in the drab colors of the post war years. It seemed then that bright colors were non-existent among most working class people. They always seemed to wear brown, gray or black and the women would wear navy blue or black.

The interior of most flats and houses, had dark green and brown paintwork. This made the memories of the time, even more dark, gloomy and so depressive. Our flat was dim, enveloped as it was in poor light, due to the ineffective gas lighting and there was not a bathroom to the property however the flat was eventually to get electricity.

My father must have been hungry that morning, for we had just turned the corner away from the flats, when with a gentle, "Whoa," he pulled Queenie to a halt, outside a pie and mash shop. "We'll go into Manze's and get something to eat, shall we?" I smiled and nodded in agreement. He put Queenie's nose-bag on her, so that she too had something to eat.

He lifted me down and as we went inside, I remember to this day, the wonderful smell, of so many hot pies. "Hello Jack," a man called out, "I'll be with you in a half a mo." "That's alright Frank, take your time," said my father. "We are but two hungry fugitives," and he looked at me, then he started to laugh. Frank appeared, "What would you like to eat Jack, and what can I get this other poor fugitive?" They both started to laugh, for he evidently, was used to my father calling in, for it seemed that he always did this, after my mother had given him a hard time. "Just the usual please Frank, and an extra mug, my little one can share with me."

Frank brought in a small plate and a teacup with some milk in it. My father poured some tea from his mug into the teacup, he then put a small pie and mash portion from his plate onto mine and Frank brought in a sweet for me too. I was as hungry as my father was that day and we both felt much better after eating our fill. Never before in my short life, had I ever felt so full and content, for I wasn't used to this. I was always hungry and starving most of the time and the little food I did get at home, was in no way nutritious and although I was chubby, this was due to a diet of fat and sugar. My father and I, both said thank you to Frank, as we left Manze's pie and mash shop.

Placing me back on the seat of the cart, he then climbed up beside me and took hold of the reins. Queenie knew exactly where she was going, for she made her way steadily across Creek Bridge towards Deptford. Once over the bridge my father pointed out the several different places. I could smell the newly cut timber before it was pointed out to me. "That's the timber yard," he said, "They call it Edwards and over there is a barge, that takes the timber to the yard by the river Thames." "And that over there my little tuppence, is the London Spinning Company, where they make the ropes, for the ships." I instinctively knew that one day, I would be working in the offices of these companies, that were pointed out to me by my father.

Once back in the stable yard, I watched as Queenie had her nosebag put on, with some fresh food for her to munch. I vividly remember the smell of the hay, as Queenie contentedly munched away, while my father proceeded to unharness her. He then gave me a brush to keep me occupied. "Now you just brush Queenie's feet for me my little tuppence," he said. I had formed a psychic link once

Fight Back To Eternity

again with this huge Shire horse, "It's alright, I will not harm you," her thoughts relayed to me. Queenie was so placid and so calm, I felt no sense of fear, as I brushed her massive feet, even though she could have crushed me to death so easily. When he had finished putting away the cart, my father placed me on top of Queenie's back, so that I could watch him work. "Look tuppence, I am going to make Queenie some new shoes." My father explained step by step, exactly what he was doing. I was mesmerized as the metal started glowing and changed color, it went from ridged to soft, just as he said it would, with sparks flying in all directions, as he fashioned it on the anvil with his hammer. Whist he concentrated on the task at hand, he still took the trouble to explain in detail, all his actions, each and every step of the making of this horseshoe. My father explained exactly what he was doing and why. He then lifted me down to watch, as he tried the shoe on Queenie's foot for size. To this day, if asked to do so, I could relate the whole process of making a horseshoe and the consequential shoeing of a horse.

These happy times with my father were few and far between and I only really got to know him later, after my mother had died. I did not realize that either of us had done anything wrong, that wonderful day we spent together. I was so glad he took me with him that day, for it was such a happy and enjoyable event, in total contrast to my existence at home, that I can still remember it vividly to this day. I enjoyed being with my father, as he always tried to cheer me up, for he must have known that my mother, gave me such a hard time at home.

One day he came home, with a small stuffed black Scottie dog. He realized that he had never seen me, with a teddy or a toy and looked on, as tears of happiness rolled down my little face but what he failed to comprehend, was that they were also tinged, with tears of sadness. I knew the minute he had gone that my mother would not let me keep it. I was right, for the moment the front door closed and he had gone out, my mother snatched it from me. "Give me that filthy thing here," she shouted, throwing it on the kitchen fire. "You're not having that, now get in that bedroom, you ugly cuss of a kid." Again I didn't know what I had done wrong, how could I? aged three.

During these times at Rockfield House, there were constant rows and my father seemed to go out, just as soon as the rows started, no doubt for his own safety. Most of the time, I could only peep through the keyhole of the bedroom door, then only if the key was not left in the lock, on the other side of the door. On seeing or hearing him leave, I always wished that I could go with him. I remember, it was at these times of loneliness and utter despair that my Heavenly Parents would send Spirit children, to comfort and play with me.

The room that I occupied, had cream distempered walls, with brown paintwork. There were no pictures or books, and there was a complete lack of stimulation, as there were no toys whatsoever. My diet was poor, as I was treated so differently from my sister. I was given bread and sugar, bread and dripping, or oxo gravy and bread. This was my normal diet, yes, bread certainly was, my staff of life. There was very little food about, after the war and I always seemed to be the one, to get the scraps, for unlike Oliver, I dare not ask for more. I became very ill, and so undernourished that it was only then, was I given cod liver oil and orange juice but only if and when my mother felt like it, or found the time to even bother. This I later understood, was given freely to those parents, with children under five after the war, as lack of food and rationing was still commonplace, in the early 50's.

Added to all this, during the 50's, Greenwich was in flood. A young man came into the room, and I didn't know who he in fact was, at the time. However, I later found out that he was my half brother Richard, who was fifteen years older than I. After stacking what little furniture there was onto the table, he waded through the water to collect me out of my sodden cot. He picked me up and carried me upstairs to a neighbor's flat, belonging to the mother of his best friend.

It seemed my twin sister, was taken earlier to an aunt in Essex, along with my brother Chris, who was five years older than my sister and I. They had all been taken to safety, with my mother, apparently leaving me behind, to whatever fate befell me. As the young man carried me up the concrete stairs, I could see the water he was wading in was jet black, as it lapped over the bottom step. Once on the first floor, he carried me into the neighbors flat and I heard him say that he had to go. He was having to put sand bags against the gates, to try to hold the raging river Thames at bay. "It isn't the first time this has happened, and it won't be the last, for there is a history of flooding in this area," I overheard him say, just as he was leaving.

Once he had left, this lovely lady started to chat to me, having observed me looking wide eyed at various things, which were dotted around on her shelves. I started asking what they were called and she kindly explained to me, what ornaments were, what books and toys were etc. For not having seen such things before, I was completely oblivious of their very existence. I explained, that we had very little in the way of furniture or ornaments. Neither were there any toys, pictures or books to be seen in the flat. There was just the one old rickety and dilapidated chair, a table and one bed also two cots. She then explained to me, as I pointed to these things, what they were called and that the small figures were also called ornaments. I then asked her, to tell me the name of the young man, who had brought me here and she was amazed and shocked that I didn't know. She said, "That young man, is in fact your half brother child, didn't you know?" I just shook my head, for I was feeling so unloved and dejected.

When my mother eventually came to collect me, she already looked angry. Once again I thought that I had done something very wrong, but I did not know what. The neighbor then began to relate, what I had said. My mother tried to say, that I had made this all up and that I was a habitual liar, but the neighbor said to her, "At this age madam, children only tell the truth." Angrily, my mother made a quick exit, roughly dragging me behind her and when we got to the top of the concrete stairs, she tried to push me down them. However mercifully, my Spirit Parents intervened, I was levitated and placed ever so gently at the bottom of the stairs, totally unharmed, with the water having subsided by then. My mother was absolutely amazed and astounded, by the realization, that there was something surreal going on.

CHAPTER 3
MY MOTHER'S REALIZATION OF MY PSYCHIC ABILITY

Following this episode, she would make me use clairvoyance, asking questions about other people. On one particular occasion, she pointed to a certain woman and asked if she was going to die and if so when? I replied, "Yes, within the week" and this came to pass, with this happening on many other occasions, which were always correctly prophesied. Eventually when she persisted in asking the same questions, over and over again, I refused to answer, for by now, I was blaming myself for their deaths, when they occurred. Malnutrition and damp living conditions, contributed to deceases like rheumatic fever, bronchial pneumonia, with death seeming, such a commonplace occurrence then. It was at this time I started getting high temperatures and nightmares, due to being under nourished. The nightmares, were of me as a young child and I was always looking down into a pit. These contained souls, who had perished in the holocaust and they would give me their names. They said, remember me to my family, for one day they will contact you, although I didn't quite understand, how this could possibly be.

One morning, a gypsy woman knocked on the door. My mother went to the door and opened it. "What do you want?" She asked in a very rude and nasty manner. "Buy some lucky heather lady ?" as I was standing right behind my mother, I mimed to the gypsy, "She's going out, call back later," this the gypsy did. I apologized for my mother being so rude to her. "I only have two old penny's please take them, keep the heather, I'm so sorry I don't have sixpence to give you." The gypsy then said something strange. "You young lady have night mares don't you?" I said, "Yes, how did you know?" She replied, "The departed contact you, they require you to do work for them, for you are very special, you have the gift. One day my child, you will know how to use this gift." She turned and walked away, giving me a wave and a lovely smile.

Following the episode, when my mother tried to throw me down the stairs, she would starve me much more than usual and I would go into a trance. She would then get the answers to her questions that way. Looking back, I feel that she would have made a lot of money, out of my psychic abilities, whilst I however, received no recompense whatsoever. She spent virtually every penny, on the greyhound racing at Catford stadium, placing bets with the bookie's runners and any money remaining went on bingo.

CHAPTER 4
DISCOVERING MY RELATIVES AND EVENTS SURROUNDING THEM

I was later to find out, that I also had a half sister by the name of Wendy, whose name was changed to Wilma on adoption. My mother had given Wilma to her eldest brother Wilfred, who had married a cousin, as they had no children of their own. I was told that she we was unable to cope, after the birth of my own brother Chris. When my sister and I were added to the family, this must have compounded the situation.

My mother would always say, "I wish you had never been born," this always being directed towards me, not my twin. I did not realize at the time, that I had a half brother and sister, who were both apparently treated, far better than I ever was. Richard and Wendy were by my mother's first marriage to John Edward Simpson, who was a representative, for a local firm. One day he was involved in an accident, when a car shunted into the back of the van he was driving. John was thrown forward, and his head hit the car windscreen. The blow to the head caused a brain tumor, John my mother's first husband, died not long after the diagnosis, that he had a brain tumor. This left Richard aged three and Wendy aged three months, for their mother to raise alone.

My mother married for a second time to my father, after she became pregnant, with their only son Chris, who looked nothing like my father, for he had dark black hair. My father had red hair and there was no resemblance whatsoever. In fact Chris looked more like, my mother's eldest brother Wilfred, who was later to adopt Wendy and change her name to Wilma. It must have been quite a shock to my mother, becoming pregnant again five years later, with twins. Father had apparently gone out drinking, with my mother and her sister Rebecca one night. I later found out that Rebecca and my mother, had become pregnant within the same year, both with twins.

I was not allowed to mix with any of the family, for I was always alone in my bedroom. However I did not mind this at all, for Spirit children would come and play with me. At one time, there was a large oak wardrobe in the room, which someone had given my mother. I used to go inside the wardrobe and go into a trance like state and this allowed me to travel into a different world. The world I traveled to had sunshine, green fields and children that I would play with. However my mother got angry, that I would use this wardrobe as a place of retreat. I would escape from this awful, vicious woman, whom I was led to believe, was my biological mother, so one day she just chopped it up and used it for firewood.

CHAPTER 5
NURSERY SCHOOL BECKONS

Aged three my twin and I, were taken to a nursery school, near Blackwell Lane in Greenwich. I remember going through the gate and my twin skipping off happily, to play with the other children. My mother held onto my hand and said to the nursery assistant, "Watch this one, she might try and make her way out of the gate." I was roughly taken inside to a cloakroom and told to hang up my coat, on the peg with the picture of a squirrel alongside it. My sister was told to hang hers on the peg, opposite the elephant picture. "Can you reach it for me?" she ever so sweetly asked. The assistant hung it up for her, then left me to try and figure out, what a bloody squirrel looked like. By the time the nursery assistant had come back, I still had not done this, as I had never seen a squirrel before in my life. There weren't any squirrels in the slums around London. Perhaps Hitler had killed them all off, however the nursery assistant, thought that I had deliberately disobeyed her. From there, I was then taken to a place, where they kept green canvas, fold up beds. I was wound in a dark gray wool blanket, so tightly that I could not move my arms or legs and I lay there, until it was time to go home.

Another assistant came and told me to get up, "I can't move," I cried. "Whoever did this to you child?" she asked. "The lady who met my mother at the gate," I replied. The Nursery assistant had to stand me up and unwind the blanket from around me, making me feel like a spinning top. I was so dizzy and when I was collected along with my sister, I felt so tearful and unhappy.

The next episode was when my sister and I were taken to St. Peters Creek Road School. I clearly remember being dropped off there. My sister Pam, wouldn't even sit next to me, making me feel like a leper or an outcast. This was exactly the way I was treated, throughout my early childhood. I was dressed in dirty second hand clothing and wore old shoes, which were far too small for me. They were bought from market stalls, in the rougher areas of Deptford and I caught skin infections because of this.

I was placed next to a boy, who was very sexually aware and kept exposing himself, I didn't quite know what was going on. The teacher yanked him roughly from his seat and took him out of the class, with his little penis still exposed, on view to all and sundry. I told my mother about it, however she said that it didn't matter, we would not be going back there anyway, as we were moving soon.

CHAPTER 6
DISCOVERING THE OUTSIDE WORLD AGE FOUR

When I was just four years old, my mother went out for the afternoon, leaving me alone as usual. Once she had gone, I left the flat and made my way to Greenwich market. There was a man, sweeping up around boxes of bananas, outside the warehouse. I looked longingly at these bananas and told him that I was so very hungry. I asked him, if he could please let me have the one on the floor, that he had just swept up. You can't eat that, it's all black and slimy. Looking down at me, he saw the disappointment on my face and realized then, that I was indeed starving. It was obvious that I didn't get much at home, this in itself being an understatement. He patted me on the head and then kindly gave me a bag full of bananas, I thanked him very much and left.

I could see a Church not far from the market, St. Alfege's Church. My research confirmed, that there had been a church here, for over a thousand years. It was dedicated to the memory of

Alfege, the Archbishop of Canterbury, who was martyred on this site in 1012. The present church is nearly 300 years old and replaced an earlier medieval building. It was the shadow, I could see of this medieval church, with my clairvoyant vision. I walked towards the Church and past the ancient gravestones, at the back of the Church. As I walked on for a short distance, I came across some swings and a slide. Sitting down, I ate what I could manage of the bananas, knowing that once I reached home, they would be taken from me. I played there for a while on my own, when I suddenly realized that It was going to get dark very soon. So I made my way back through the Churchyard and on looking down, found two old penny's on the ground.

It was unbelievable, the only luck that I had ever had before, in my short life so far, had all been bad and I wondered if the gypsy had dropped them there. On picking up the two old penny's, I made my way down the narrow cobbled back streets, as there was a shop there, which appeared to be open. Thinking I could buy some sweets to hide away and eat when I was really hungry, as I so often was, I went in. The bell rang, above the door as I entered, pushing the door fully open, that had been left slightly ajar. Carefully I walked in and once inside, I could see a very high counter, with empty brown shelves above. The three people in the shop, turned their heads to look at me. A man whom I can only describe now, as looking like Abraham Lincoln, was very stern, gray and menacing. Next to him were standing two ladies, both wearing gray silk dresses with bonnets. It was then, that I had an overwhelming sense of fear and ran home from that shop, as fast as I could. We had no television then, so how had I perceived such a scene, for I had never been shown a book, at that time either. Looking back, I believe I must have somehow traveled back in time, or so it would seem, for I can envisage no other explanation.

On arriving home and finding that there was no one around, I put myself to bed, as there was nothing else for me to do. When I awoke next morning, the bananas had gone from the kitchen and my mother asked me, where I had got them from and I told her. She didn't seem to mind, or to even care that I had gone out alone, or that anything could have happened to me. I recall after this episode, my mother sending me out, to ask the local shopkeepers for scraps. One being the fish monger, the other being the man at the Greenwich market, who had been kind enough, to let me have the bananas. Another time, I was sent out with a pair of men's pajamas to sell, they were folded up in plain brown paper. I was told which door to knock on and to ask sixpence, for the pajamas. The neighbor, after much pleading from me, finally bought them. Whilst on one of these begging missions, I went back along the old cobbled path to where the strange shop was standing, where I had seen the gentleman with the tall hat who resembled Abraham Lincoln and his two lady companions. However that shop wasn't there, how had I managed to go into this shop, this puzzled me.

The following afternoon, a man dressed in an American's sailor's uniform, knocked on the door. My mother half opened the door, with me standing just behind her and of course my sister Pam, was in front of her. He had a broad smile and was tall and good looking, with tanned skin, and sharp features. The sailor said that there was a battle ship, moored in the Thames and they were calling, from door to door. They wanted to give the children in the area, an early Christmas party, I personally had no idea, what a party even was. My mother said, that my sister Pam could go, he then asked, "What about the other little girl?" "No, she's not well enough," she said, pushing me back along the passageway. So it was, that my sister got to go and have a great time, whilst I was not even allowed to see, what clothes she would wear for the party.

It would appear that I was the original Cinderella, for I was told, "Stay in the bedroom or else." With the or else, meaning that I would be plunged into a tin bath of hot water. The water was always far too hot, however If I cried, she would slap me, so I learned not to cry and just go out of body, until it was all over.

On my sister Pam's return, I could see that she had a good time, her face was full of smiles. The American Sailor had given her a doll in a beautiful case. The case was dark blue like the night sky, with little silver stars that sparkled. The Sailor had included one for me, he had shown a kindness toward me, knowing how disappointed I was, not having been allowed to go. I remember to this day that my case, being the same as Pam's, was covered in little silver stars. It was the most beautiful thing, I had ever seen in my life, the doll was so lovely.

My sister Pam's was even more beautiful than mine, for her doll had a pretty red dress and bonnet. I remember saying to Pam, that our mother would be taking them from us. We would not have the dolls to keep, very long, as there was no way, that we could hide them. We only had the dolls for a couple of days, for my mother took them away, whilst we were asleep and sold them.

One Sunday, my mother took me to a tin hut and left, saying that I would be collected in a couple of hours. To my surprise other children started to arrive and there was a rather short man called Ted, who announced that he would be taking Sunday school. I was sitting at the front, so I had a clear view of a felt board, on which he placed cut out figures, also made of felt. Later in life, I realized that this must have been to do with Palm Sunday. I had the privilege of placing the felt donkey, on the picture board. He then said that there was some one called Jesus, who he prayed to on a regular basis. Everyone in the class, was asked to put their hands up, if they also believed in Jesus. Looking around me I could see that no one had put their hand up, so I raised mine. I could see a beautiful light, encircling this man, with an angel standing alongside him, so to me this was proof, that there was a more beautiful place and that Jesus was real. The prayer that I was taught that day, stayed with me for the rest of my life. Whenever I was afraid of the dark or had a nightmare, I would say this prayer and it would make me feel so much better. The words in the prayer were for protection and guidance.

CHAPTER 7
THE SCHOOL INSPECTOR CALLS

Fast approaching five, I was told that we would soon be moving. One day my mother went out in the morning, taking my sister with her. As she invariably did this, I had come to accept it, as being normal. My mother's parting words were, "Remember don't answer the door to anyone, or else."

She had not been gone long, when there was a knock at the door, thinking that she had come back for something, I opened the door. There stood an exceptionally tall man, peering down at me, over the top of his glasses, looking very stern. "Is your mother in?" he asked. "No she's not," I replied. "Are you Pam Dodson?" with a shake of my head I said, "No, she left with my mother." "Then who are you?" he asked. "My name is Penny" I replied. "Well, I don't seem to have you down here on my list at all."

I asked who he was, he ignored me and merely replied. "Tell your mother that it has been reported, that Pam has not been attending preschool, also tell her, that she has to register you for school as well and as soon as possible." He told me, that he would be back to have a word with my mother and I was to tell her that he was from the school board. On my mother's return, I related what had been said and told her that he would be calling to see her and that he said he would be checking up on her. My mother was seething, for she was already in a bad mood, as she had lost all her money on the dogs and now this, on top of everything else. She said that I would be going to bed hungry and I thought, well there's nothing unusual there and being such a regular occurrence, it no longer bothered me. Not long after this, the man from the school board came back to visit again. "Why did you only register the one girl?" he asked. "Where is Penny?" I want to see her now, Mrs Dodson and I mean this very minute." "She's not well enough," my mother retorted. I overheard every word, as I was standing just behind her, so my mother, who was totally unaware that I was just behind her said, "Penny is unable to come to the door she's very ill," thinking I was still locked in the bedroom. "Just step to one side Madam," he said to my mother. "You're Penny aren't you?" I just nodded and smiled and he could see that all my baby teeth were black. This made him even angrier and he shouted, "Have you never taken this child to see a dentist?" My mother said, "No and what's that got to do, with her going to school anyway?" "I strongly suggest, that you make an appointment with the school dentist and before she starts school at five years old, so don't forget." He then thrust the address of the dentist into her hand saying, "I shall be back to check up on you, madam."

I was roughly escorted along to the school dentist, shortly after this conversation and I was given gas with the entire front and side teeth extracted, whilst I was under. The dentist asked if I brushed my teeth regularly and I said that I had never even seen a tooth brush in my life before. Once more I could see the anger welling up in my mother. "Is this true, your child has never been given a tooth brush before?" he asked. The dentist then gave me a Mickey Mouse toothbrush and some toothpaste, telling me to brush the teeth at the back, as these few teeth he had managed to save, I had no idea who Mickey Mouse was, or even what he looked like, however I noticed, that he had bigger ears than me. Just as I had no idea, until later in life that my sister had been able to attend a street party, for the Coronation of the Queen. Such was my isolation and lack of contact with the outside world.

As my second teeth started to come through, I would brush them. I had to ask my father to buy me a toothbrush, for after the first one wore out, my mother refused to do so. I was also refused toothpaste and told to brush my teeth with soot and salt.

CHAPTER 8
MOTHER GOES ON NIGHT SHIFT LEAVING US ON OUR OWN

One night my mother announced, that she had a job, which would bring in a little extra money. This job she proudly informed us was piecework and involved working night shift. It was sorting rags at the local rag factory, which was called Dandridge's, mother went on to say that it was a big factory, opposite the soap works in Deptford. For once my twin was around, this meant that I would not be in the flat on my own.

My father had not been home in ages, for if he had, then I must have been asleep, when he came. I was always told, that I had to go to my room at six pm and not to come out until morning. The room was always cold and damp and the walls were bare, with the windows on the inside, having ice on them. I used to sleep in my clothes, as it was too cold to take them off. Even though there were no books or toys, I was always glad to go to my room. This meant that I could play with the Spirit children and escape from the drabness of this world. On the first night my mother went to work, after proudly telling us, she would return in the morning. Her parting words were, we must not answer the door or tell our father that she had a job working nights. There were just the two of us alone in this dismal flat and to make sure that we didn't use the electricity, she took the light bulbs out. My sister would have normally been taken, to stay with my aunt Rebecca, however I guess my mother thought, that she dared not chance leaving me all night, in the flat alone.

Pam related a story that night, after first stating that she would have rather gone to stay with aunt Rebecca, than be with me. She explained that aunt Rebecca had two daughters the same age we were, one she had let go for adoption. There was a photo of the two little baby girls, on the sideboard, these girls belonged to aunt Rebecca. I didn't quite comprehend what my sister Pam was talking about but listened anyway. It seemed that aunt Rebecca who's husband had died, just after aunt Rebecca became pregnant. Pam went on to explain, that in the photo one of the two baby girls had died, within two weeks of being born, with the other apparently adopted out, to one of the family. It later transpired, I was in fact that child, adopted by my mother and father, for he was in fact my biological father. He had got both my mother and her sister Rebecca pregnant, within the same year. As Rebecca and my mother were very much alike, I was the replacement, for the twin girl my mother had lost. This was around the same time that aunt Rebecca lost her baby girl. I later realized that this fully explained, why the person that I had always assumed to be my biological mother, had such an intense animosity and hatred, towards both my father and I.

CHAPTER 9
OUR FIRST DAY OUT AS A FAMILY

My half brother Chris, was sent to a boarding school at Royston, courtesy of the newly formed NHS in 1948. Chris had stopped growing and the Doctor felt that the fresh air of an open air school, would be the answer to the health issues he had. One Sunday, there was an open day at the school in Royston and for the first time ever, aged five, my sister Pam and I went to visit, along with my parents. This journey was the first time in my life, that I had traveled on a train. We walked to Greenwich Rail Station and boarded a train to New Cross, from there we traveled into London Bridge Station. There were people rushing here and there, but after a short time however, we eventually boarded a train from London to Royston. On our arrival at Royston station, the sky was a bright blue and the air was clean and fresh and I felt comfortable, warmed by the summer sunshine. Royston station was decorated with tubs, made from old beer barrels, with all the tubs containing a range of pretty flowers.

The different colors, made the tubs look resplendent, in the rays of the summer sun and the scent from these flowers, smelt so lovely.

I said to my father that I was very thirsty, for it was a long journey and no one had thought to bring a drink along. The Stationmaster on hearing this said, "Don't worry they can have some water from the tap inside my office." which I thought was very kind of him. He gave my sister and I a cup of water each and then said, "Help yourselves if you need some more." The water tasted clean and it had a different taste to the water in Greenwich. We were dressed decently for a change and to the outside world, must have seemed like a normal family. My father asked directions from the stationmaster and on leaving the station, we turned left and were soon walking down a country lane. I remember the warm sunshine on my face and the lovely fresh smell of the countryside. I felt so happy to be outside, encompassed in a totally different environment.

On arrival at Royston School, Hertfordshire, we all stood in awe of such a beautiful and magnificent building, which at one time, must have been a grand stately home. A master met my parents at the gate and they were taken inside, with my sister and I both being told to go and play, which we happily did, for I was eager to explore the beautiful gardens. I had never been anywhere with both my parents before and the place was a mansion, with beautiful lawns, which appeared to stretch for miles. There were large tents on the lawns and I could see that there were tables inside. I overheard a lady saying, that the marquees must have taken ages to set up. Inside the marquees, the tables were laden with cakes and sandwiches of all kinds. I remember thinking, if only I could escape to a place like this.

My parents and my brother Chris, who looked really well and was dressed smartly in his school uniform, eventually joined us. The fresh air, surrounding the location of this school, must have done the trick, for he appeared to have grown during the time he had spent there. Good food and a great environment, would have contributed towards this remarkable change in him. I also remember, getting a glimpse of people, who would have lived there, prior to the mansion being turned into a school, it must have been the previous occupants, for they were not dressed in the costume of the current time.

It wasn't the taste of the cakes that I remembered on this wonderful day out, but the taste of the fresh clean drinking water. This was strange, you would have expected, that it would have been the other way around.

A voice said "You will be able to visit beautiful places like this one day, however until then, you will have many trials to go through, for much work will be required at your hands." "However your footsteps will be guided, also there will be inspired promptings, from beyond the Veil." My Ethereal Parents were communicating with me once more, for they had not abandoned me.

My half brother Richard, was in the Royal Air Force, being trained as a flight instructor, with this being funded, by the family of my mother's first husband.

CHAPTER 10
RE-LOCATING TO MY FINAL RESIDENCE WITH THE FAMILY

On the day we moved, when I was five years old, there was a lot of rushing about. My father was busy loading, what few items there were, onto the cart. My sister had already gone ahead and I had a large heavy meat platter to hold, as I walked behind my mother. With arms outstretched, trying to hold on to this meat platter, I was made to walk the three quarter mile to the next block of flats. I walked the entire length of the Royal Naval College, pleading with her to take the platter from me. She just turned to me saying, "Shut up moaning you ugly cuss, just you keep up or else."

Not wanting to get into hot water as it were, I tried to keep up, as she meant this literally. The flat had three bedrooms and appeared more spacious than the one we had just left. This one was situated on the penultimate floor, from the very top of the flats. There was no lift and I could not carry this platter any further, so I dropped it.

So this was to be my next prison

It was not long after moving into this flat that I became really ill. My mother had dragged an old mattress, along with an iron bedstead, out of the air raid shelter and I was made to lie on this. The room which I now occupied, was cold and damp, as there was no central heating then. The flats were prewar, sited opposite, what was then, the old Greenwich power station. This made for an even more unhealthy environment. The tall black chimneys, belched out great plumes of black smoke, on a daily basis and this must have all added, to the thick yellow smog that hung in the air.

The only patch of green grass to be seen, was the lawn in front of the Greenwich retirement home. This retirement home was situated, just alongside the towering power station, which was built tall enough, to overshadow anything that was situated just beneath. This power station was the only other view to the flat, I thought even as a child that the retirement home, was not a very healthy place to retire to, for the ex power workers. I later understood, that the constant burning of coal, would have given those who lived through the smog and grime at that time, in the south east of London, a much shorter life span.

A few weeks after laying on the filthy mattress, which as previously mentioned, had been dragged from the air raid shelter, I became desperately ill. I was not only covered in boils, due to a poor diet, but had scabs all over my scalp and I also had bouts of tonsillitis on a regular basis. Being too weak to move, I was washed and cleaned up and then dressed in a white nightdress. I had never even seen a nightdress before, let alone ever worn one. My father lifted me out of the bed and I was placed into a room, the door of which, I had previously been forbidden to open. Once inside, there was a warm fire burning in the hearth and a large double bed with fresh white sheets, that were spotlessly clean, over which was a beautiful white satin bed cover. I wondered who occupied, such a room as this. It was like being in a completely different world, to the one that I had always been used to. Not long after this, a lady dressed in a district nurses uniform arrived. Whilst I can describe this to the reader now, at that time I was just told, that a lady was coming to see to me. I was given penicillin injections on a daily basis for two weeks. Following this treatment, I was pulled out of the warm bed and pushed back into the room, I had been taken from. I eventually got better, as my Heavenly Parents intervened, by levitating me above the bed and making the bed army style, for it was the bed bugs, from this mattress, that had contributed to making me so ill.

After complaining to my mother, about these hard backed bugs crawling over me, she did nothing about it, she merely shouted, "It's just your stupid imagination, you'll get the back of my hand if you keep going on." "If you won't believe me, lay on it tonight yourself," I said defiantly. "It's the last time that you will make me lay on this bed ever again." A voice said, "Go and get a knife, cut open the mattress" and this I did. Before too long, the whole room was alive with brown hard backed bed bugs. These bugs came teaming out from the mattress, along with bits of broken glass. These bits of glass had been blasted inside, by one of Hitler's bombs, that had been dropped during an air raid. This mattress, must have been at least ten years old, for it had been in the air raid shelter long before I was born. This had all been inside the mattress, that I had been laying on. "What did you do that for?" was all my mother could scream. She then dragged the filthy mattress out onto the landing and proceeded to cut it up. Those horrible bed bugs were crawling everywhere, with my mother trying as quickly as possible, to stuff bits of the mattress down the rubbish shoot. The neighbor's passing by, made comments like "Don't block the rubbish shoot now, will you Mrs Dodson?"

Bliss, I no longer had to wake up, with those creepy bugs crawling over me. "Thank you so much my Heavenly Parents, for once again you have come to my rescue."

CHAPTER 11
MY FIRST TASTE OF FREEDOM

Once I had started to stand up to my mother, my life became a little bit easier and I was allowed out. On one occasion, after my sister Pam had been bullied by a gang of boys, she came to me for help. I don't know how I managed to summon up the courage, as I confronted the bully. He left her alone after that and even let us join in, playing a game called cannon. You had to try and knock the top off, what looked like a cricket stump with a ball, leaving the other stumps of fire stick, still standing.

My Heavenly Parents must have decided, more distance was needed and a number of events started to unfold. "Leave the flats," they said. "Just go round the corner." I found myself in a narrow alley, on one side a public house called the Yacht and on the other, a row of old terraced houses. Walking over the cobbled stones, I was painfully aware of just how hard they were, through my thin soled shoes. I was directed towards the River Thames, where at the top of the alley, I found myself outside a huge house that was painted a creamy yellow. This house is now called the Trafalgar Tavern. Through my research,

I discovered that the Trafalgar Tavern was built on the site of the Old George Inn, during the reign of Queen Victoria, 1837. However during the 1950's, this became a very large private residence, which later became a bar and restaurant. I could see children playing outside and I was invited to play with them and whilst we were playing outside, a lady appeared. She had a pretty face and a lovely smile and the children must have been her son and daughter. She said they had just moved in and then turned and went inside. However a little while later, she came out with some lemonade and biscuits. Oh how I wish I had an earthly mother like this, I thought to myself. It started to rain, "Come inside and play, children, before you get too wet and your new friend can come in, for a while also but she has to go home, when it has stopped raining."

Once inside, I could see that there was a large bay window that overlooked the river Thames. There were lots of ships sailing by, on turning around, I could see a large ornate green onyx and gold round table, with carvings on the legs. Two gentlemen were looking at maps, which they had spread out over the table. They were, as I am now aware, dressed in the costume of Nelson's era. They seemed completely unaware, that children were playing around them. I was amazed that the little girl could see them too, for I could see, that she was staring at them, with great fascination. When the little girl turned to me and said, "Can you see the two gentlemen?" I nodded. Her brother said, that she was just making things up, when she mentioned this to him. "Stop trying to scare me you silly girl, I'll tell mother!"

Their mother on hearing raised voices, came to see what was going on. "What are you two arguing about now?" she asked, "Helen has been telling ghost stories again," her son said. "Now just stop trying to scare your brother Helen, tell your friend it's stopped raining and she must go home now." I turned and thanked them and started to go, taking one last look at the green onyx table. I could see the two gentlemen at the table, who were in the dark blue uniform of Nelson's flagship, waving at me. My last glimpse, was of the sumptuous, large gilded staircase, which gently curved up toward the rooms above, it was fully carpeted in red. This beautiful building had bay windows going right the way up, with the exception of the very top floor. These windows, would all have had a picturesque view, over the river Thames and today I understand, there is a statue of Lord Nelson outside.

My Heavenly Parents told me, "One day you will visit more beautiful places, until that time, you have many trials to go through," this statement they had made before. I retraced my footsteps, following the cobble stones, back along the alleyway, with the cobble stones looking so black and shiny, still wet following the heavy rain. My Heavenly Parents seemed to be giving me a strong message. "You have many trials yet to come and these trials will strengthen you, for life's journey, whilst you will be given much, a lot will be required to be performed at your hands, however with inspired promptings, your pathway will become clear."

I looked to the left of me and halfway along the alley, there was an iron gate. A lady was undoing the chain and I was prompted to follow her in. On glancing around, I perceived two large wooden barrels, standing by the backdoor of the Inn. A couple of tables and chairs were strategically placed, to take in the view over the Thames. These tables and chairs, were all fashioned from old beer barrels. The lady came out, asking if she could help me. "I wondered if you might have any jobs?" I inquired. She smiled saying, "Well I think you may be a bit young, to work here my dear, don't you?" I found myself prompted to say, "It's not for me, it's for my mum." "Well we do have a vacancy, for someone willing to collect and wash the glasses," she said. "We are very busy most evenings and weekends, tell her to come at six tonight and she's got the job, I admire someone like you, who has initiative."

I made my way back towards the flats and as they came in to view, the red brick looked even more old and dismal than usual. They too, like the cobble stones, still held some of the signs, of the recent heavy rain.

CHAPTER 12
I MAKE FRIENDS AND GET MY MOTHER EMPLOYMENT

I remember there were two girls, both looking out over the wall in my direction. "Hello, we haven't seen you before, are you new around here?" "No," I replied. "I've never really been allowed to venture this way before." "My name's Linda," said the eldest one of the two. "My names Lucy," said the younger girl. "What's your name?" "I'm Penny," I replied. "Would you like to be our friend?" they asked. "Thanks for asking, yes that would be good, I can't stop now though, would the same time tomorrow be alright?" I could hardly believe it, twice in one day I had made new friends

When I arrived home I could hear my mother complaining. "I don't have a job now to go to." So I piped up, "Mum I have only just spoken to someone, a lady who said that she was looking to hire someone to collect and wash the glasses, at the Yacht Inn." I went on to say that having spoken to this lady, she'd told me that if you went round at six this evening, you would get the job. My mother couldn't believe her luck, so this she subsequently did and got the job.

My mother didn't bother with babysitters, as the last time she paid someone to keep an eye on us, we were made to sit on a cold stone step and not invited into the neighbor's house. We had to sit there, whilst they had their dinner and all my sister and I could do, was sit and look at the rain, until my mother returned. When she did, I told her what had been happening and asked, "Why do we have to sit on a cold doorstep, in the wind and rain everyday, until you return?" Mother asked, had we not ever been invited in. "No," my sister and I replied. I suggested that we wait outside our own flat, rather than this ground floor door step. After we had related what was going on, we heard our mother shouting, "I'm paying you good money to look after them," meaning my sister and I. "And you don't even invite them into the passage out of the cold, I've been told that, you have never so much as offered them a drink of water, let alone something to eat." "You only asked me to keep an eye on them and this I did." was the reply. So thank goodness, we did not have to suffer the cold, on this neighbor's doorstep and being treated like stray dogs.

The fact that my mother was out every night, working at the Yacht Inn, gave me the freedom to play and explore. I soon became very firm friends with Linda and Lucy, for though my twin was staying in the flat more, we never really played together. Pam had her own set of friends, in school and out. Thanks to my sister, I never made any friends at school and was often in trouble. Pam would tell them not to play with me, making some derogatory remark or other, about me. She would tell the teacher, that I copied from her book, for at every opportunity, she would try to get me into trouble, in order for her, not to have to sit next to me. I was often punished, at both school and home because of her, for Pam could charm the birds out of the trees and had become a very accomplished liar. My sister would always try and humiliate me, in front of her friends, "This is my sister but she's not very bright, she's backward you know." These were the sort of nasty comments, she made all the time and I always seemed to lose new found friends, because of this. It wasn't long, before I lost Linda and Lucy's friendship and whilst my sister was made welcome, whenever she went to play with them, I no longer was. What had happened, how had the situation changed? They had been my friends, but now for some reason, only Pam was allowed to play with them, Why?

CHAPTER 13
I LEAVE MY BODY AND THE EARTHLY PLANE

At the age of around nine, my back teeth had started to deteriorate and having pulled out two of them myself, I was still in need of a dentist, to attend to the other two, as they were broken and quite decayed.

Consequently, an appointment was made with the school dentist, with both my mother and sister coming along with me, for they knew that I didn't want to go. The dentist was, as I know now, from Pakistan and I was lifted into the chair. A rubber wedge was pushed firmly, into my mouth, I struggled and protested, "Stop, Stop," I screamed. The nurse held me down, whilst the dentist held the gas mask, firmly over my face. I could hear a bang, bang, like the noise of a drum in my head, for the beating of my heart sounded so loud. I drifted towards the light and once in the light, there was a circle of people dressed in white robes. My entire life thus far, flashed by like sub titles.

I observed a gold bench, I felt very tired and desperately wanted to lay down on this bench. I knew that once I did, I would have no memory of the Earth plane. I instinctively knew that I had to try and hold on to one memory, of the Earthly experience. This I desperately tried to do, trying to hold on to one of the life memories, flashing before me. I knew, that if I could not hold on to one memory of this world, that I would have no recollection at all of the Earth Plane. The only memory I had was that of fear and this bought me back to the Earth plane. Fear is the heaviest of vibrations, for if you have no negative thoughts, then you will go swiftly into the light.

I stood in the circle of the White Robed ones and addressed them saying, "I had to go back, I had special work to do," these were my parting words to them. So it was the memory of fear, that helped me return to the earth plane. On my return back, I found myself standing outside the door of the room, where my body lay still and lifeless. Still out of body, I could see my mother and sister sitting in the waiting area, just outside the door of the dental surgery. My mother and sister, realizing something serious had happened, were shouting at the dental Nurse, as she rushed passed them wheeling a large oxygen cylinder, into the dental surgery. I followed, walking straight through the door without having to open it. Seeing my body laying white and lifeless in the chair, I knew that I must get back into my body immediately.

I could hear my mother shouting and screaming at the dentist, I came round with the oxygen mask firmly over my face. When fully conscious, I was helped down out of the dentist chair. Once on my feet, my mother pushed me out of the surgery door, as if it was entirely all my fault, shouting, "You're never going back to a dentist ever again," and whilst she was alive, I never did, I had to wait till I was fifteen.

CHAPTER 14
MY FIRST THREE WEEKS AWAY FROM HOME

During the time at Aylmer house, my mother had various jobs and I was always glad of the peace and quiet, when she wasn't around.

At one point my sister Pam went to stay with aunt Rebecca and I went to stay with my aunt Maud in Brightlingsea Essex. This was the first time I had seen them. Rebecca and Maud were my mother's two sisters, they had such nice homes and good food on the table everyday, why was my mother so different from them?

This was another small taste of freedom and staying there in the countryside, with the sea front so close by, was so wonderful for me. It held memories, of when I played with the Spirit children inside the oak wardrobe. Just to experience a near normal childhood, whilst enforcing my love of the countryside and the sea, was a wonderful experience at this time.

I would go for a walk down to the harbor and enjoy, the fresh smell of the salt air, intermingled with that of the seaweed, that came wafting in from the open sea. I would spend hours looking out to sea, watching the fishing boats, coming in and out. I wondered what it would be like, to live this kind of life, even though it appeared to be a hard existence. Also I clearly remember, the wonderful smell of the shrimps. These were being cooked by the fishermen, alongside their boats, which were moored by the harbor, at Brightlingsea sea front. I quickly learned, that if I stood around talking to them long enough, they would offer me some shrimps, which I relished with the utmost satisfaction. Not far from the harbor, was situated the old bric-a-brac shop, or should I say antique's shop, which I loved to explore. These antique items were really a training ground, for my Spiritual development. When I handled the objects, I could sometimes pick up the story, surrounding these objects and see whom they once belonged to, for knowledge is given when one is alone, in the silence.

I picked up one particular small carved elephant in ivory and admired the exquisite detail and elaborate workmanship. I was able to perceive the person whose name, was quietly whispered to me as Ranie, who had carved the elephant. Ranie was sitting cross legged in the dust and sweltering heat. Ranie looked to be, a good looking Indian man, in his late twenties, he was sheltered under a canopy just above him, no doubt to alleviate the rays of the hot sun. He was carving small objects also from ivory, to be sold as souvenirs. Ranie worked with such obvious dedication. This was understandable, as Spirit told me this was his only means of making a living, to feed and clothe himself and his family. I also touched an authentic spinning wheel, not a reproduction and had a vision of a small elderly Scottish woman, toiling away, whilst quietly singing.

Close by, where I was staying, with my aunt Maud and her family, was a small farm and I was sent to buy some eggs for my aunt. The lady who approached me, was wearing a long flowing black dress, with a white apron. She asked, did I want a lot of yolks in them and I said yes, wondering exactly what she meant. She explained that the first basket of eggs, only had one yolk in each one, the next basket had two and another three. So I asked her was she Psychic, she said no, I weigh each egg and can then tell how many yolks are in them. I didn't really believe her but felt it would not be polite to say so. I asked for eggs that all had three yolks and took them back to my aunt Maud. Sure enough each egg, when cracked open, had three yolks, as she had predicted, I found this to be uncanny to say the least. My aunt said the lady had never been wrong before.

On a night, my aunt Maud, uncle John, their sons and I, would play cards and I remember one card game called chase the Ace. We also played domino's, snakes and ladders and tidily winks. There were no televisions or computers around at this time, so people made their own entertainment.

The day too quickly came, when I reluctantly, had to say goodbye to my aunt Maud and return home, knowing also that I would never see them again.

CHAPTER 15
SECONDARY AND IT'S LOW GRADE EDUCATION SYSTEM

The day came too quickly, when I had to return home to Greenwich, to the smog and the grime and constant rows. I felt that this childhood was such a dark unpleasant time back in Greenwich. My mother gambled and my father was a heavy drinker, it was no wonder that we were poor.

I was told that I would be going to school with my sister Pam, to the school opposite the flats where we lived. The school was called the Meridian school. However to start with, we were sent to a school, which was miles away from where we lived, as there were no places at the time in the Meridian school. The school we were first to attend was called Buridge Grove school, in Plumpstead, Woolwich. We were there for just a few days, as the Buridge Grove school, was full of gangs and bullies. They sought me out for some reason, on the very first day. My sister Pam made a quick exit from the classroom, leaving me wondering what was going on. A gang of these girls burst in blocking my way out. They asked, "You the new girl?" I looked at them in shock, knowing they meant me harm. These girls, who I had never laid eyes on before, pinned my hand to the desk and gouged great lumps out of it. On my return home, I explained to my mother what had taken place, showing her my hand. where it was gouged and to this day, it still has a scar. How could children be so cruel to another child, who was a stranger and in the school for the very first day? I said to my mother, that I would never return there, however I was made to go but I attended only for a few days. After this I never returned, the school was just too dangerous. However, this was just the beginning of the cruel acts I would witness, during my time spent in this low grade school system.

On arrival at the Meridian school, which was walking distance from the flats, we were made to put school benches in a row, in the assembly hall. I thought it was for a school assembly. A boy introduced himself to me, as Johnny Williams. He approached me and asked me a favor, I didn't know him, as it was my first day. "What is it? you look terrified." "Can you ask the headmaster, if before he does the mass beatings, will he let me keep my trousers on?" "My family are very poor and my mother couldn't afford to buy underpants for me." Feeling sick to my stomach, I don't know how I plucked up the courage that first day, to approach the headmaster, who's name was Mr Raven. He was a tall, very strict man, with jet-black hair. "Mr Raven, this is my first day at this school and Johnny has just told me, that his mother could not afford to buy him underpants, so would you please let him keep his trousers on, when you cane him?" Mr Raven, looked at me, possibly thinking this young child has courage, for he agreed to do so. The caning of these boys was so cruel and unjust, however at this school, it seemed to be a regular occurrence. Where was the care that should have been shown to these children? Most were from poor families and were undernourished.

After the war, I found out in later life, that those from the forces, had been recruited as teachers, regardless of their character or abilities. I was so traumatized, not only at school but at home too, so much so that I withdrew within myself. Also I had bad eyesight, due to having been on such a poor diet for so long, with measles also adding to this. I was made to sit at the back of the class, unable to see anything that the teacher wrote on the black board and having withdrawn within myself, I no longer cared. Eventually I had difficulty with my speech and I was placed in a deaf and dumb class. All I can remember of this school, was not only the cruelty and horror of it all but also the trauma, which was compounded by the lack of care at home.

It was at this time, that I recall my mother being constantly in and out of hospital. When she was at home, I used to have to get up in the middle of the night, in order to take care of her. My father was often home late and in the early hours, I would often find him slumped in the toilet, asleep on the floor. To save the rows between my mother and father, I would listen out for him and help to get him out of the toilet, after having woken him up.

The next school, we were obliged to attend, was Greenwich Park Central, a secondary school. Life was a little easier here, for by this time I was classified as backward. No one took the time or trouble, to investigate as to what the cause really was and with my stammer being made fun of, this didn't help either. Greenwich Park Central Secondary school was situated on the other side of the Royal Naval College Greenwich. I would walk through Greenwich Park on my way to school everyday. I enjoyed the beautiful park, with it's bird songs and flowers. I could see the General Wolfe statue, at the top of the hill, by the Royal Observatory. As I walked by the Queen's House, also known as the Greenwich Museum, with my clairvoyant vision, I could see the shadows of the servants in past times, running to and fro, with

Fight Back To Eternity

huge dishes laden with food and large jugs, which looked to be wine or water jugs. The space they ran through, was open to the elements and looked across to the Royal Naval College. On looking towards the hill again, the one that supports the General James Wolfe statue, I thought what a great man he must have been. My research in later life, informed me that General James Wolfe commanded the British forces at Quebec, against the French and won a great victory, at the cost of his own life. He was born in the year 1727, January 2nd and died in 1759, 13th September. A British Army Officer noted for his strict training and remembered for the battle against the French in Quebec. Being a resident of Greenwich, he was buried in the parish church St. Alfege's. On a personal note, I was born in Greenwich and confirmed by the Archbishop of Southwark, in the parish church of St. Alfege. Looking once more towards the hill, on which the General James Wolfe statue is mounted, I observed an opening, beneath the hill that opened up into a tunnel. With my clairvoyant vision, I could see that these tunnels went for miles and there was even a tunnel, that went under the Greenwich Museum too. This must have been very useful, for those who wished to escape. Spirit informed me that the tunnels just beneath the hill, where the General James Wolfe statue stood, went toward a place called Chislehurst. I explored the park more after school and there was an entrance to the park, from the Maze hill side. As I walked through Greenwich Park, one beautiful summer afternoon, I came across a very ancient tree. With my Etheric vision having a greater power, than the physical vision, I would often use this as an additional aid. Many of the phenomena of the physical world, may be examined, as may also many creatures, of a non-human nature, which are ordinarily, just outside the range of the physical vision. This vision responds readily, to stimuli of various kinds and becomes active under their influence.

The tree had a seat inside the hollow and I could see the Etheric double, of Queen Ann, who loved to sit there and read or embroider and just get away from her courtiers. The tree gave her shelter from the rain, and shade from the sun. The next day after seeing the Etheric body of Queen Ann, sitting inside the old tree in Greenwich Park, I was to have yet another Spiritual encounter with my Heavenly Parents. It was whilst attending a cookery class, at Greenwich Park Central school and after being asked to write my date of birth and address, that I went into shock. This was sparked off, by the very fact that I had no idea, when my date of birth in fact actually was, so I asked with a stammer, if I could be excused to go home early, as I felt unwell. The teacher agreed to let me leave early that afternoon. The sudden realization, of not even knowing my date of birth, made all this too much and I went as white as a sheet and could not even remember my way home. I got to the school gate and could not recollect where I even lived, or which way to go. Thankfully my Heavenly Parents came to my rescue again and I was Spiritually guided back home. I remember getting on a bus, that must have been close to the school and that I lived, somewhere near the Royal Naval College but I was unable to remember, which side of the Royal Naval College I lived. I explained this to the bus conductor, telling him that I was suffering from shock. He stopped the bus at every stop, so that I might see something, which may be familiar to me. I said to the bus conductor that I still could not remember the stop, I was supposed to get off at. He kindly said that this is the last stop, after the Royal Naval College and wished me good luck. And so I disembarked, hoping I could find my way back home, from the end of the Royal Naval College. My Heavenly Parents took over, once I alighted from the bus. "Go to the left" they said. "Then cross over the road, walk straight on," and they directed me back to the flat.

I confronted my mother, once I had recovered enough to do so. Why have you never shown me a birth certificate?" I asked but she just ignored the question. "Why have you never shown me a birth certificate?" I demanded once again. "You will get into trouble with the school, I will go to the head and let them know that you have refused this request." "I don't know where it is," she stated. However after a couple of days, she thrust the certificate into my hands and it was then and only then, that I discovered that I was born at Easter, toward the end of March.

CHAPTER 16
LEAVING SCHOOL AND THE DEATH OF MY MOTHER

At this stage of my education, or lack of, I just waited for the day to leave school. At the age of fourteen, everyone of this age group, was asked to see the headmistress, for a work reference. As my education was almost non existent she kindly wrote, Penelope can perform any task, to the best of her ability. Ability, what ability?

I left this low grade school system at fourteen, for it was pointless, going back. All I could remember, was this great sense of relief, at leaving such a substandard school system.

I was about to get up early, the morning after leaving school at fourteen, to go and look for a job. As I looked up toward the bedroom door, I perceived a tall dark and sinister shadow approach me and I said my special prayer of protection that I had learned when I was three years of age and I asked it to leave. This dark being, or energy turned and entered my mother's room. I had an immense feeling of horror, having witnessed this event. Shortly after this, my mother suffered a stroke and an ambulance was called. My mother was taken into St Alfege's hospital. My research in later life showed, that this had been formerly a workhouse in 1723.

My sister Pam, or should I say half sister and I, were astonished to see how skeletal looking, our mother had become. When pulling back the sheet, we could see mother curled in a tight ball, nothing more than skin and bones. I knew then, that this was the last time, I or my half sister Pam would ever see her alive. My father never visited her, as she had given him such a hard time. All that negative energy, was in the home as I was growing up. Thank goodness I used prayer for protection and guidance, whilst I was growing up in such a negative environment.

We were informed by our next door neighbor, who took a message over the phone, that our mother died shortly after our visit, for she never regained consciousness. I was never able to find the answers, to the many questions, which I so desperately needed to know, one being how Pam's real twin had died after being born, also how the other twin of aunt Rebecca, had passed away too. Why had aunt Rebecca given me over, to be a a replacement for the child, my mother had lost, which would have been Pam's birth twin and so it was I was the replacement for this twin.

Why was I not allowed to see aunt Rebecca, for Rebecca was my biological mother. All these questions were left unanswered. Rebecca and the person that I had been led to believe was my mother, were very much alike and my father was our biological father, this explained, why Pam and I looked very much like each other too.

All I had to go on, was a handful of certificates, which I had been prompted to hide as a child. These I had retrieved, when my mother had been busily burning certificates, one afternoon. The day my mother died, must have been a relief for my father, for each day had been fraught with arguments, screaming and shouting, consequently there was never any fun or laughter within our flat. I could count on one hand, the amount of times we went out as a family and there were never any holidays as a family. The only break was when aunt Maud had looked after me for a short time, neither were there any birthday celebrations. Christmas was never celebrated, books, toys or any other stimulus, were absent from this flat. As my mother treated me as a non-existent child, she would only talk to me, if it were unavoidable to do otherwise. There were very little if any, happy memories regarding my mother. Instead of sadness, I felt relieved that she had passed on. Later on in life when in my thirties, I was able to do the ordinance for her, in the Latter Day Saints Temple. Her Spirit followed me home that day and I had to tell her to go into the light and be at peace, for I had forgiven her.

I had been out looking for work and on my return my father was sat at the table. This had been his usual repose, since my mother had died. He would sit there for hours just looking into his newspaper and just stopping to roll a cigarette, in his little machine. He turned to me and said that he couldn't bring himself to make the arrangements for the funeral. "Would you take care of it he asked?" So age fourteen, I had to try and find out the procedure, for making the arrangements, regarding a cremation.

I walked the length of the Royal Naval College, passing the iron black railings and then St Alfege's Church. I had just reached the Greenwich Town hall, there must have been a German bomber that fired at this clock tower, for I could see it's shadow, firing directly at the clock tower, just as it must have done in the war years. Walking by the Town Hall clock tower, I could see my half brother Richard. Richard was driving along in his gray Morris van, for after Richard finished his time, in the Royal Air Force, he became a rep for a local firm, just like his father John had done. I waved Richard to stop, which he reluctantly did. "What do you want?" He demanded curtly. "Did you know that mother has died?" I asked. "No, what do you want me to do about it?" He asked. Richard should have been the one, making the arrangements for the funeral. I was fourteen and he was twenty nine, I would not be fifteen until the end of March. "Please Richard, just tell me how to go on." "Go over there to the DHSS for the grant, then go a couple of doors up to the undertaker, they will arrange the rest," he said and then just drove off without a care in the world, I guess at this point in his life, he was going up the ladder in life and he had also become a Freemason. I was just a half sister from the slums, that he'd rather not even acknowledge. However I followed these instructions and made all the arrangements, much to the surprise of the undertaker. He could not believe that there was no one other than me, capable of making the funeral arrangements. The undertaker asked, if the body once collected from the hospital, would be remaining with them, until the cremation. I did not hesitate and explained that the flat, was second from the top floor and that there were no lifts. I said that I felt it would be better, that the body of my mother, go straight to the crematorium from the undertakers. "Please send someone to collect the wreaths and floral tributes on the day though, thank you." With this, the undertaker turned to me and inquired, "How old are you?" "I am fourteen." I replied. "I am sorry that you have had to be the only one, to make the arrangements for your mother." I said that I realized, death as being part of life and that dying is ceasing to be afraid. I thanked him for his help and left.

Back at home, I placed all the wreaths, which were sent by neighbors and relatives in the bath, as the bathroom, was the coldest room in the flat. Many of the flowers, were sent from people, that I had never even heard of. My father hadn't a clue what to do, when the wreaths started arriving, he went into a flap, saying, "Where are we going to put all these wreaths?" When I couldn't place anymore of the wreaths inside the bath, I had my father take off the cupboard door and used this to accommodate the rest of the wreaths, by placing the door over the bath. As stated, the bathroom was the coldest room in the flat and it was excellent for keeping the flowers fresh. On looking at all these beautiful flowers, I felt sad that my mother never had flowers given to her, when she was alive. I instructed the undertakers when they called, just to collect the flowers from the flat and asked them to place the wreaths in with the coffin, as the hearse carrying my mother, would be parked outside the grounds of the flat. There was just the one limo, which followed behind the coffin and there was just my sister Pam and I in the limo. My father didn't want to attend the funeral, so there was just my sister and I at the crematorium too. I had to make all the arrangements for the ashes and had them scattered at the crematorium, in the garden of remembrance. Then I made arrangements for my mother's name, to be placed in the book of remembrance. I had done all I could, at this present time and could do no more.

On reaching home after the funeral, I felt drained but I had learned not to show emotion a long time ago. My father met us at the door and said, "Thank you for taking care of things." In the very next sentence, he said, that my sister and I would have to go out to work. "I'm not able to work because of my heart condition," for years of drinking had taken its toll on his health. "Why don't you go and register at Robertson's jam factory?" he asked.

I knew what I wanted and so I replied, "I don't want to work in a factory, I want to work in an office." "You have had very little education," he said. Those with Gypsy connections back then, did not believe in educating girls, some schools also gave the boys at that time, a better education than the girls. The family will never talk to you ever again, they will think you are a snob," he said. I replied, "I have never even met, all your family, so why should I care, what they think of me now?"

CHAPTER 17
LOOKING FOR EMPLOYMENT

I took any job that came along, carving ham in Sainsburys on a Saturday morning, working in a cinema on an evening as a usherette. When the lights went out, you had to walk backwards, showing people to their seats. One of my other jobs was selling ice cream, however there was a gang of children at that time, who were adept at stealing. So at the end of the day, as this was taken out of my pay, there was no point in carrying on with that particular job.

Just before I was fifteen, I was prompted to go and ask for work, at Marks and Spencer, located in Deptford high street. I approached a tall lady, who stood very upright, she explained to me that she had terrible back pain and so had to wear a steel corset, due to a problem with her spine. "I am so sorry to hear that you are in pain, I hope that you feel better soon!" She must have warmed to me, because of this sympathetic remark.

"Excuse me, " I asked as politely as I could. "Would you know if there are any work vacancies here?" She smiled, "Well, you've asked the right person, I'm the Manageress." "How old are you? you look as if you should still be at school." "I'm nearly fifteen." I replied, "I will be fifteen at Easter and I really need a job, as there is very little in the way of meals at home." "Well come back when you are fifteen, if you pass the math test, I will give you a job."

I cheated and went back, two weeks before my fifteenth birthday and though my spelling was still poor then, my mental arithmetic was very good. I had managed to master the art of adding and subtraction in my head, as there was a lack of writing material in the flat. On my arrival there, the manageress took me upstairs and I was given two full sheets of paper with maths questions on. I did the whole lot within ten minutes, without getting one wrong and I was given the job straight away. The Manageress then asked, "Do you get enough to eat at home?" This question initially took me by surprise, as I had forgotten that I had mentioned this, during our first conversation, when I had asked if there were any vacancies. "No," I said. She then turned to the lady in the canteen and said, "Give this young lady a lunch for free plus a sweet and if she wants anymore to eat before she leaves, she shall have it." Also she informed her, "When this young lady starts work on Monday, if ever she wants seconds, you are not to charge her, there is to be no charge for the first week." As promised for the first week I received my meals for free.

I started work at 8.30. am and finished at 7 p.m. The lady in charge of the canteen then said, that it would be better if I paid for my meals as soon as possible, as the other staff members would deem it as favoritism. Once eating properly and on a regular basis, my brain became more attentive and active. I was able to retain knowledge easily.

I walked the two miles to work every day and back, to save money and I was still only fourteen, when I earned my first weeks wage. In my pay packet was a five pound note and this I had to hand to my father, who gave me back one pound. I worked six days a week, for just one pound.

I was glad that we had to wear overalls, for on starting work I only had the one dress. I managed to save up ten shillings to buy material and make shift dresses, as these were the fashion at the time in the sixties. As I only weighed six stone, shift dresses were easy, just straight up each side, hem and hey presto, job done. There were at that time, a range of psychedelic colors, which were very trendy. I managed to keep up with fashion, in this way. As time went by, I got a little more confident and made myself a jacket and a coat. I bought an old treadle Singer sewing machine for a pound. I would buy a second hand coat, have it cleaned, take it apart, use an up to date modern pattern and construct the latest fashionable coat or jacket. Marks and Spencer would let the staff buy returns for 2 shillings, this being 10p in to days currency, so here again I manged to buy cardigans, baby doll pajamas and trendy lingerie.

Eventually I saved enough money, to take a course at the South East London College. I had not given up my idea, of working in an office, so enrolled in a course for Pittman's Short hand and typing. On passing, I then went on to do an English course. Whilst attending the college, I made a friend, called Melissa, who was from Cyprus.

Melissa had yet to perfect her English, so I would help her with this and in turn, I learned to read and write and speak Greek. I stayed friends with Melissa for some years. I also managed to rescue her, from where she was living, for she was made to work in her uncle's shop, after she had finished work. Melissa stated that she was made to sleep on the kitchen floor. She was not paid by her uncle, for the work she did in the shop either. I took Melissa to get a student benefit, so that she could be independent and have the funds to rent a bed sit. This Melissa did and was able to get the best out of her education.

CHAPTER 18

MY FIRST LOVE

I met my first love, whilst working at Marks and Spencer in Deptford, when I was still fifteen. Ralph was the cousin of the shop porter Dave, who had asked me, if I would make up a foursome after work, one Saturday night. They were planning a trip to Ramsgate and Dave said that his cousin Ralph, would like to meet me. Ralph was five years older then me and was training to be a Quantity Surveyor.

This first date was an exciting time for me, as I had only ever known work, home and college and that was only when, I could afford the fee for night school. I had also led a very sheltered life, before this time of relative freedom. I asked my father if I could go and explained that the night out was work related. As my father was going to one of the many family party's, with his eldest brother, this was no problem. I must also explain that I had never been included in any family party's, on either my father's or mother's side of the family. I was raised in complete isolation from any normal family life. The only family event, was my half brother's wedding but even then, I was not included, in the group wedding photos.

I was collected straight from work and was wearing a pretty shift dress, which I had made that week and a brand new white cardigan, which I had just purchased from Marks and Spencer for the princely sum of two shillings, or ten pence in new currency. For once I felt special. Ralph was a lovely man and we got on from the start. As I had changed at work, I met Ralph outside the shop. Ralph and I got into the car with his cousin and we all went to Ramsgate, where I had the best time ever, for we laughed and joked a lot. There is always a song that reminds you, of a special time. The song for me, which was playing on the car radio that Saturday evening, was "Sweets for my sweet, sugar for my honey." Every time I hear this tune, it reminds me of that trip to Ramsgate.

Ralph and his cousin, who had a great looking girl friend called Daisy, played cards every other Saturday and I was invited along on the second date. They explained that the game was called poker, so I said that as I had never played cards, in this gambling sense, I would just watch. They all started to laugh, as they were about to play strip poker.

Ralph's cousin Dave, who had introduced me to Ralph and I can say with all honesty, looked very much like Elvis Presley, especially the way he combed his jet black hair. Dave's girl friend looked like a model. Daisy had her hair piled high, in the Beaufort style. Ralph's sister June, also had come along to the gathering, with her boyfriend who was also called Dave, only June's Dave had red hair. They called him Dave Red, so as not to get confused when playing cards. The Dave who resembled Elvis Presley, they would refer to as Dave Black, so there were three males and three females. I was thinking at this point that I should leave, as Dave, Daisy's boyfriend smoked heavy and drank neat whiskey, as all the males started drinking too, I wanted to make a quick exit. They did offer me a drink but I had to refuse, as I had never drank alcohol before in my life. I was about to get up and leave, after saying I wasn't comfortable with the situation, when they all decided that perhaps it wasn't the right thing to do. After all, I was still only fifteen and they were all in their early twenty's.

I knew at this time that I had a lot more freedom, as my mother had passed on and my father was not around that much, as he went to his sister most days. I guess that she provided his food for him, for the cupboards were always empty at home, so unless I managed to buy some food, to take home and cook, there was nothing else on the menu, on a daily basis. Thank goodness I could purchase a meal at work, for six pence.

Ralph eventually took me home to meet his parents, who lived on Peppy's estate in Deptford, this had just been built. Ralph's mother asked me to join them, every night for a meal, which was very kind of her. Ralph had told them about my home circumstances and that I had to hand over, almost all of my pay to my father. Ralph had explained that I only got the one meal a day, from the canteen at work. Ralph's mother smiled and said, "You look like you could do with feeding up, how much do you weigh?" "Six stone," I replied.

Their flat was a large modern sprawling flat and was very nicely carpeted, with deep green carpet. The flat had bedrooms upstairs and down on the ground floor, there was a door off the kitchen, leading on to a small garden. I had never seen anything so warm and welcoming, for Ralph's family were lovely.

Their uncle Oswald lived with them and he had been with the family, since being liberated from a Japanese prisoner of war camp. He showed me his shins, which had deep ridges cut into them, where his flesh had been carved away. One day shortly after meeting him, he went on to explain to me, that in the Japanese Prison Camp, he had contracted a decease, known as Beriberi. This was a consequence of his captivity in the Far East. Oswald went on to say, that it was caused by a deficiency of vitamin B1, this was also a thiamine deficiency disease, all this was explained to him later, by a doctor. Oswald related to me, that it was prevalent in Eastern countries that had a basic diet, of just white rice and the disease beriberi he explained, was common in the prison camp. Uncle Oswald added, that the Far East was a place, that he would never recommend to anyone. The Japanese he said, used to call Beriberi, Kakke. The only cure was to cut it out with a knife, Oswald had used his penknife and this saved his life.

However shortly after meeting Ralph's uncle Oswald, he passed away with Cancer. I went into his room to see him, just before he died and I could see his Spirit departing from his body. On my way out, I could see Oswald's Spirit form on the stairs, looking fit and well. Oswald smiled and waved to me, he looked such a tall and noble young man, not like the older man, who had just past away.

CHAPTER 19
MY FATHER EVICTS MY SISTER

During this time, I never had much to do with my sister Pam, as she was nearly always out and I never knew where she went to either. Pam was always in and out, being very smartly dressed and was able to find money for new clothes, on a regular basis. My father said that Pam was always borrowing money from him and not paying him back. Perhaps if we had been allowed to keep £2, instead of just £1 from our wage, Pam would not have had to borrow in the first place. Arriving home one day from work, I asked my father where Pam was, but all my father would say was that he had enough of the way Pam carried on and had told her to get out and not to come back. I had no idea where Pam had gone to live. It must have been hard for her, to find herself suddenly on the street, at fifteen years of age. However Pam dropped by at the flat one day, when my father was out, saying that she needed to collect some things. Pam was abusive and laughing and began to push me. I knew nothing about drugs or personality disorders, or other labels that went along with abnormal behavior but I managed to say to her, look we are both nearly sixteen, you must start to behave like an adult. You can't just come here and start pushing me around, punching me and wanting to fight, as if you are a demented child, venting your anger. And so it was, that she agreed not to carry on with this behavior, I went on to say that neither of us had any chance, of a normal upbringing, for we had never even celebrated a birthday together. I suggested that we put the past behind us and turn things around for the better. At my suggestion, we agreed to meet up, on our sixteenth birthday and give each other our first birthday card, together with a small present. We met up on our sixteenth birthday and celebrated together, with a cream cake and two small candles. Pam and I gave each other a card and a present. This was the very first time ever, that I had received a birthday card, let alone a birthday present. We agreed not to fight or argue, as I explained to Pam that because of our upbringing, we should put all that aside. Pam was not very close to my father, so this made things very difficult between them and consequently, on my return home from work one night, as previously mentioned, Pam was nowhere to be seen. I repeatedly asked my father where he thought Pam may have gone to, as I had searched everywhere and had no news of Pam. My father just said without any emotion, "I've told her to leave and not come back!" adding, "I don't want to talk about it anymore."

Pam I know, liked to go out a lot and never said where she had been, or where she was going. I was informed some time later that Pam was sharing a flat with her friend Tessa, whose step-mother had put her out also, for whatever reason. Pam as stated earlier, always managed to dress smartly. This had always puzzled me, as she could not possibly have afforded, the smart shop bought clothes, on a teenager's wage. She would never tell me exactly, what sort of employment she had, except to say she had got a job, as a receptionist. I was told at this time, by one of Ralph's other cousins, that my sister Pam had been seen, in areas that were not so good. Things must have been very difficult for her, having to live in such an insecure way.

One Saturday, a green sports car drew up outside the flats, driven by a rather handsome young man, by the name of Simon and alongside him, sat my sister Pam. Simon had a fresh young complexion but he also had a darkness about him. With his smart modern dress sense, good looks and sports car, would have appeared a good catch but I sensed that his soul qualities were not good.

It was shortly after, that Pam announced aged eighteen, that she needed my father's signature to get married. Simon was a very quiet man and I felt very uneasy around him, so when my sister was cooking dinner for him, I asked her, "Do you really want to marry him?" Pam seemed to have no idea whatsoever, that he wasn't going to be the one in her life for long and I tried to explain this to her. She just said that I was jealous, because he had a sports car but this didn't bother me at all, I was just genuinely concerned for her. Sometimes, when you are too close to a situation, to quote a metaphor, you are unable to see the wood, for the trees.

My father and I attended the wedding, which was held at the Town Hall in Greenwich. I didn't go to the reception, as my father and I, were not invited. I was glad, as I knew she would try and humiliate me, by telling people that I was not very bright. I had never explained to Pam that by going to college on a night, for the past three years, I was no longer the much maligned and dim-witted person, of the past. I had not been to a disco at this time, as my intentions were, finally to establish a good education for myself. I knew Pam would tell people that I was old fashioned and square, which was the same, as not being cool today. My father did not want to attend the reception either, he went off to another family party, after the wedding ceremony. I went home, changed, and went out to a dance with Ralph, the dance being held at the Ballroom, which was situated at the top floor, of Burton's Taylor's in Greenwich. Ralph and I were both learning Ball room dancing, at the time,

CHAPTER 20

I CONTINUE WITH MY SELF EDUCATION

I finally managed to save enough money, to continue to self educate myself at this late stage in my life. My spelling really improved, from that day forward and I discovered the wonderful world of books. I applied to take a test for the GPO Avenue Exchange, near Billingsgate in London and amazed myself, by passing the stringent spelling test. I was trained on the huge dolls eye switchboard, that they had at the time. I had to stand on a box, to put the plug in, at the highest point of the switchboard. Everything was done by hand, even the writing of the tickets, which were pale green or buff yellow. As stated, we had to write these out by hand and they told you, how much was spent on each phone call. If the caller asked for an ADC, this meant you had to call them back, to advise of the duration and charge of the call. At that time, we also took a turn, on operating the Royal switchboard and whilst the pay was better, it was an earlier start. I would walk through Billingsgate fish market, at 5 a.m. each morning, this meant me leaving home at 4 a.m. I remember seeing a huge ray fish, laying on the cobbled floor one morning and I thought, what a beautiful creature and could visualize it, in it's natural environment.

The mornings I walked through Billingsgate Market, were dark and very cold. Whilst these men worked in extreme cold at the fish market, they were always friendly and cheerful. I really enjoyed walking through each morning and I looked forward to my work. They were a great crowd of people to work with, also it gave me more money, to carry on with my studies. I studied Pittman's short hand, for I wanted to eventually work as a short hand typist, I learned book keeping too.

One of my work placements on leaving the GPO, was the London Spinning Company in Deptford and the other being Edwards timber company. Both of these company's were situated near Creek bridge. These company's were pointed out to me, by my father when I was three years old.

My career led me onwards and upwards, for in the late sixty's to seventy's, it was so easy to walk in and out of a job. You could be earning £10 a week in the morning and then following an interview during the lunch hour, start a new job the following week, making fifteen pounds. I remember going for an interview at Lloyd's of London shipping company. The Manager who interviewed me, must have really wanted me to work there. He wrote me a romantic letter, asking if he could take me out, which I declined. At the time, I was earning far more than my father's basic wage, when he was employed, however I never told him this. I started working for a Stock Brokers, where I worked for six years, receiving a bonus of around a thousand pounds, twice a year.

The teenage years were fun, for I was making new friends and mixing in circles with Ralph, that I could only have dreamed of. At this stage in my life, I was discovering new places and getting to go on holiday with friends. My first holiday, was a week on the Norfolk broads, which was a lot of fun with lovely scenery. We moored the boat, dressed up and went across the fields, to find a country inn. We found one, it was like stepping into someone's front room, for it had a log fire and a bar on one side of the room. There were people playing dominoes and one elderly gentleman, who had string tied around his coat, looked like someone, who had just stepped out of the eighteenth century. We settled ourselves down and the landlord said, "I'm just going to buy some fish and chips, would you four, like me to purchase some, for you too?" "Yes please" we all replied in unison. Not one of us knew where we were, for we had just stumbled on this place, more by good luck, than good judgment. I enjoyed this holiday so much, for I had never experienced such carefree times.

CHAPTER 21
A CLOSE ENCOUNTER

Ralph had passed his exams and had a lot of rich clients at Edwards, near Waterloo where he worked. Ralph bought himself a red MGTC sports car, which gave us the freedom to get out and about. On one of our excursions, we went through a tunnel and were almost half way through, when a huge lorry was coming straight at us, head on. The lorry had been in the wrong lane and had driven into the wrong side of the tunnel. Ralph and I looked at each other, knowing that we could not possibly survive and we both said goodbye, at the same time.

Once again, my Heavenly Parents came to my rescue, for on opening our eyes, we found ourselves on the outside of the tunnel, totally unharmed. We looked at each other, in absolute astonishment, as there was no way, could we avoid the oncoming lorry. It would have been impossible, for the sports car to go under the wagon, as the trailer was low to the ground. We never spoke of this paranormal episode again, for it was so spooky that Ralph and I, could not bring ourselves to talk about it. I had never told him of my Heavenly Parents, who had rescued me on numerous occasions. Ralph sold the sports car, after what should have been a fatal accident, possibly due to the shock, following this harrowing experience. My clairvoyance kicked in and I sensed, that we would not marry, for I knew that Ralph and his cousin Dave would not have a long earthly life and my predictions came true, as they always did. I was encouraged by Ralph and his family to carry on studying.

I learned to drive at seventeen, the very first instructor I had, said that I would never make a driver, as I had no road sense. So I saved enough to go with BSM and try again, buying a block of twenty lessons for just £20. The Driving instructor I first had, was a bad tempered man with a handle bar mustache. He was red faced and must have been used to heavy drinking, as he was very over weight too. However the next instructor, had a calm, well-balanced personality and put me at ease straight away. He even put a marker in the middle of the back window, so that I could align the car perfectly when reversing. The instructor put blocks under the seat, to raise it a little, as I was diminutive, with my weight still low, for I had only managed to put on half a stone, in spite of eating more. When I sat in the drivers seat, I was just at the right height to get a good view, of all the blind spots, around the car. As I had learned to drive in places like Trafalgar square, having to take my test in Lewisham was no problem. On the day of my test, I was so nervous that I nearly forgot where I had parked the car. As mentioned, I took the test in Lewisham and I remember doing an emergency stop, whilst heading for a fallen tree, which was in a lane lined with trees. I turned to the examiner and said, "It's a good time to say stop, don't you think?" The examiner who had not been concentrating replied, "I'm glad you told me, yes stop." My father could not believe it, when I told him that I had passed my driving test, for I had never told him that I had saved enough money, to take lessons. Neither had I told him that I had self educated myself, as I did not want him to find out and think me even more of a snob, which he had once accused me of being, for not wanting to work in a jam factory.

CHAPTER 22
FORCED TO LEAVE HOME

Though my sister Pam had married at eighteen, she divorced after two years, as her first marriage turned out to be very violent. She soon met another man called Thomas, who was much more down to earth and full of fun. He was such a really likable young man, who was a plumber by trade. I guess she must have met him one night, whilst out drinking, for they both liked a drink. By the time Pam was twenty one, she had a baby boy and he was lovely, with a mop of red hair, the same color as my father's hair. My father was delighted that he had a grandson and I guess the birth of her son, made the tension between them disappear.

The good wage I was now earning, enabled me to leave home, shortly after my brother Chris, his wife Liz and their two year old baby moved in. They were coming over from Skibbereen, County Cork in Ireland, as they had no other place to live. I had to agree with my father, for them to come and stay with us, as my father was concerned for the child.

I still carried on, giving him four pounds a week, for a long time and when my wage reached twenty pounds a week, I gave him five pounds. The twenty pounds was the basic weekly wage, with the large bonuses, giving me a very good comfortable living wage.

Shortly after Chris, his wife and their two year old son Jason arrived, life became unbearable. Liz was so ignorant that she did not even make any meals for her son and was still giving him a bottle, as his only diet. Liz had no idea about preparing food or doing the basics around the house. My father thought, I was being very generous, as by now, I found myself buying for their two year old son Jason. However things gradually got worse at home, so I decided to leave. Liz would search through all my belongings, when I was out. I would come home, to find safety boxes broken into and my private papers sifted through. Added to this my father would go to his sister's and my brother and his wife, would go out drinking every evening, leaving me to look after Jason. When my brother and his wife got home, from their night out drinking, they would fight and become very abusive. I could not bear this situation any longer, so one night I walked out, just as they both walked in the door drunk. As I had to find some where out of the rain, I made my way toward another town. I could see what looked like a quiet well run pub. I had never had the courage to walk into a pub before. This time was different, I knew I had to go inside. You know when you get that gut feeling, about something being right, this was one of those times. After ordering, I sat with a glass of orange and as I was hungry, a packet of crisps. The Hermits Cave pub, which is situated in Camberwell Green. What an apt name I thought, as I had always felt that way, with my isolated childhood A young couple sat next to me and introduced themselves as Denise and Alec. They then asked why I was looking so down and stressed out. I explained the situation at home and said that I could not bear to live there anymore. Having kindly listened to what was troubling me, they then to my surprise, offered me the two rooms in their attic.

This was for a rental of £2 a week, so I said that I would like to have a look at the rooms. They showed me the two rooms, with one being a large front room and the other a large back room. Both of these rooms were in need of decorating, however I didn't care, for I would finally have a place to call home. I spoke to my father that night and said, that I could not bear the situation at home any longer. Knowing he was unwilling to send my brother and his family back to her parents in Ireland, because of his own concern for their child, I felt that I had no alternative but to leave.

CHAPTER 23

THE ATTIC FLAT

So it was, that I moved out the following Monday, taking my bed, dressing table and wardrobe, plus my clothes and other belongings. I spent the weekend decorating and padding out the lathe and horsehair walls with paper, around the window. Then putting wall liner on and papering with wood chip, making it look quite solid. I painted the walls mustard, to give it a warm look and laid a turquoise blue carpet. I managed to buy a second hand television, a cottage style sofa and chairs. Pam's husband Thomas, who worked as a plumber, brought around a fold down table, with four mock leather covered chairs. Thomas also was kind enough, to plumb a sink unit in and put a water heater and cooker in for me on the landing. The gas meter took a shilling and would last the week. The bedroom, I carpeted with purple carpet, painting the walls white, with a hint of lilac and with the pale pink bedroom furniture and pink bed cover on the double bed, it looked very smart. I also laid a lace bedspread, on top of the pink bed cover, which made the bedroom look very luxurious. This effectively turned the two double rooms into a cozy little flat. My first home was put together, with the kindness of my brother in law and that of strangers. Thankfully, I had peace at last, a cozy place to come home to after work. However, on arriving home to my attic flat the first night, I became aware of scratching under the sink unit. I had some unwanted visitors, who were not paying rent, large rats. I had to obtain some poison to get rid of them, which thankfully proved very effective.

I quickly discovered that there were all sorts of ghosts, who once lived there. This was another spiritual learning curve, so saying prayers, I blessed the walls and the Spirit visitors, telling them that they needed to go into the light. This was my first successful attempt at exorcism, or should I say exorcisms.

As there was not a bath, in this grand looking house at the time, you had to walk across the road to the green. There was a building with public baths, which were also known as slipper baths. For six pence, you could get a large hot bathroom all to yourself, with a heated towel rail. I used to fill the bath almost to the top with bubble bath. To this, I added perfume, such heavenly luxury, that I could have only dreamed about, before then. The only down side to renting this attic flat, apart from having to get rid of the rats, was that there was no bathroom. The toilet was outside in the garden in what looked like a small cupboard. This meant going down several flights of stairs and having to put my coat on and wellingtons, if the rain was too heavy, it meant taking an umbrella too.

During this time at the flat, I worked in Portland House, as a secretary and telex typist, for a German company. I loved it, as the location was near the West End in London. I got to shop in Liberty's during the lunch hour and see all the latest fashions in Carnaby Street and to visit Harrods. This was just one of the many jobs I had, after working for Marks and Spencer and after the GPO, for I was also an accomplished telex operator. Germans work hard, and like to celebrate, so whenever it was someone's birthday, we would lock the lift, this being the only way into the office at Portland house. We would all end up in the wine bar, for the rest of the day. I would get to work really early and do all my typing before 10 a.m. as I didn't want to fall behind with my work. The company was called Klein Shanson Becker, also known as KSB. It was a great company to work for, we had good office friendships, with lots of fun too. In addition, we all had a German teacher giving us tuition, for a couple of hours a week. So I could not only read and write in German but also in Greek. For earlier at college my friend Melissa, had helped me to read and write in Greek.

After leaving home, I became good friends with the landlord and his wife, who asked me to have a drink with them, quite regularly and I got to know all their friends too. There was one by the name of Markos, who was always very friendly towards me. He was originally from Cyprus and ran his own business as a dress designer and clothing manufacturer. He showed me where he worked and he often used to bring nice coats and jackets around for me to buy, at reasonable prices.

Although Ralph was still a part of my life, we didn't see each other much, as we were both working long hours, trying to further our careers. As I divulged earlier on, I knew that I would not end up with Ralph and in fact both he and Dave, died very young. However, having known from an early age, what it was like to experience death, I knew there was definitely a life hereafter and from what I had experienced aged ten, there was a beautiful world, awaiting us.

CHAPTER 24
MY INVITATION TO ATTEND COURT

I went to see my friend Melissa, who I had made friends with at college, on several occasions, I would get a cheap flight out to Cyprus, on a weekend. This was like a mini holiday and I went to many a Greek wedding, whilst over there.

In 1973 Melissa's nephew Demetrios, came over from Cyprus for a short visit. I pretended that I already had someone in my life, when in fact at the time, I had not. He would come round with his guitar and serenade both Melissa and I with his songs, for he was a very good singer and song writer. One night I got a phone call from Melissa, saying that he was at the Elephant and Castle. Would I go and give him some assistance, as there was a problem with his car. It was 10.30 p.m. and I walked most of the way from Camberwell Green, before I managed to get the bus, to where he was parked. Demetrios, Melissa's nephew, was sitting in a white Morris, when I got off the bus and walked up to his car. I asked him what was the matter and he then asked me to get in, as it was now raining and getting colder, I did get in the passenger seat of the car. "Do you have a driving license?" he asked, "Yes, why do you ask?" Demetrios then drove off with me. "What do you think you are doing?" I again shouted at him. Before he had driven very far, there was a police car chasing us, forcing his Morris car to stop. There were two police officers in the car and they both jumped out. The policeman leaned into the car window, "Can I see your driving license?" to which Demetrios replied "I don't have a full license, officer, but she has a license." "Then can I see your license, madam?" I showed the officer my license but still was not fully aware of what was really going on. The police went all over the white Morris car, taking note of every discrepancy to do with the car, with every fault and every illegality noted down. They had just finished doing this, when Demitrios drove off once more, with me still in the car. I said to Demitrios, "Look you have to stop, let me out, you just can't drive off, away from the police, I want to know what is going on." The police caught up with the Morris car once again. They were pretty annoyed with us both, by this time, I tried to explain that Demitrios was nothing to do with me, neither was the car. I explained that his aunt had rung me, saying he needed assistance, as his car wouldn't start. Whilst Demitrios was her nephew, I did not personally know him that well, even though his aunt was one of my best friends. I felt very angry that she had put me in this situation and would be telling her straight how I felt, when I got home. The police continued to go over the car again, having taken not a bit of notice of anything that I had told them. By this time I was furious and got out of the car, the police were still checking the wheels. I had no sooner got out of the car when Demetrios sped off once more and the police jumped into their car and gave chase yet again. I walked home and it was quite late, when I arrived back at the attic flat, in Camberwell Green. I went to bed that night, utterly exhausted.

Two weeks after the incident with Demetrios, the police sent me an invitation to appear at the Tower of London Court, obviously I was extremely nervous. I told Melissa about being summoned to Court, because of the incident with her nephew Demitrios.

Melissa had just recently married, into a family of lawyers and barristers, so her new husband turned up at the Court. He met me in the waiting area, grinning from ear to ear and told me not to worry. Not to worry, worrying, I was not worrying, I was absolutely terrified that I would end up with a criminal record, through no fault of my own. A police officer advised me that there were over a hundred charges against me, saying that the police, had doubled everything they had charged us both with, because Demitrios had driven off, when the police were going over the Morris car, fault finding. The police must have doubled the charges, then multiplied each charge by ten, to reach that sort of figure. However I was the only one attending Court, that the police could pin these charges on.

After reading all the charges relating to the car, the police officer approached me and advised me that I should plead guilty, as this would make it easier for me. I replied that as I was totally innocent, I would be pleading not guilty and shortly after speaking to the police officer, I was shown into the Tower Court room. It was old fashioned with wood panels and the Judge was seated, dressed in his gown and wig, peering over the top of his glasses.

I was shown into the dock, where I felt faint and the Court room started to spin round and around. I must have gone very pale, for the Court usher quickly bought a chair for me to sit on. I could hear the Judge's voice, vaguely in the distance, "Where is the young lady concerned in this case?" "She's sat down me Lord, as she felt faint," so I was asked to stand up. Still feeling faint, I clung onto the rail. "Well," the Judge said, bright red by now. "Tell her to stand up." "She is standing up, me Lord," replied the Court usher. "Then get a chair for her to stand on!" the Judge bellowed back. "She's still feeling faint, me Lord, she might fall off." replied the Court usher. "Well get her a glass of water, and tell her to sit down," the Judge bellowed back, going even redder in the face. "How do you plead?" shouted the Judge. I replied in a quiet voice, "Not guilty Sir." "Tell her to speak up, I can't hear her." the Judge screamed. The Court usher said, "Not guilty, me Lord." The Judge then turned to the police officer and asked "Where is the young man who was driving the car?" "We don't know, me Lord," he replied looking very embarrassed. "You don't know, you don't know." shouted the Judge. "We think that he has left the country." to which the Judge spluttered, "He's done what?" "Left the country me Lord," stammered the officer, all but in tears. "And where is the car now, may I ask?" screamed the Judge. "We don't know, me Lord." replied the red faced police officer. "You don't know, how dare you waste my time, how dare you!" bellowed the Judge, his wig shaking once more with temper. "Case dismissed!" shouted the Judge, slamming his fist on the bench. I was free to go, so with my knees still knocking and feeling that they would give way at any moment, I made my way out into the foyer. There, Melissa's husband was waiting, he was grinning, as I approached him. "What happened there?" I asked him. "And where was Demitrios?" I asked, "He should have been the one facing these charges." "He went back to Cyprus." said Nickos. Melissa's husband, Nickos had just newly qualified as a Barrister, so I guess he must have been relieved too, that the Judge had thrown the case out of Court. "The Judge had no choice, but to throw the case out of Court." and with that statement, we both began to laugh. We were then asked to leave, by the same police officer, who had advised me to plead guilty. I said goodbye to Demitrios's uncle Nickos and made my way back to work and believe me when I say, I was so relieved to be back at work, free as a bird.

That afternoon it was someone's birthday at work, so the lift was closed and we all ended up in the wine bar. For once I was glad of this, as I did not feel like doing much, after the ordeal of the Courtroom.

This made a good topic of conversation though and I was also resolute, that I would never plead guilty, especially when I was innocent and being urged to do so by the police.

I made my way back that evening, to my flat in Camberwell Green, feeling so relieved that the day was finally over.

The weekend after attending the Tower Court, I had a phone call from Cyprus, asking if I would attend the wedding of Melissa's sister. It was 5 a.m. and I said that I would attend the wedding reception as I probably would not reach Cyprus, at such short notice, in time for the ceremony but would try and make the reception. I wanted to catch up with Melissa's nephew and give him a good telling off, for landing me in such trouble over the car incident.

I arrived to the airport just before 11 a.m. and managed to get a flight into Cyprus, arriving in time for the evening reception. It must be said that the family gave me a V.I.P. weekend, to make up for having found myself in trouble through Demitrios and all he had put me through, over the car incident. The reception was held in a field and I was sat next to Melissa and everyone was having a wonderful evening. The night was warm and pleasant, the sound of happy people singing and laughing together, rang out through the night. The smell of good food and wine wafted throughout this beautiful evening. I was talking to Melissa, when a man approached, who was a local celebrity, Melissa said that he was previously a simple shepherd. "You won't believe what you are about to witness," Melissa said, giving me a broad smile and no longer had Melissa made this statement, when he started to dance. Arms out stretched, he bent down to grasp the long table, which was littered with food and drink, not with his hands but holding the edge of the table in his mouth, his arms out stretched. I had never seen such an unbelievable act. I found this a bit scary, for he did not spill one glass, Melissa said that he was a professional performer.

I remembered what I had read, of the one called Akiba, who was a Jewish rabbi in the first Century. Akiba was a simple shepherd, who became a great scholar. Akiba was trying to win the hand, of a young lady he admired. The Jews said that he was a Conjurer and when he was at the height of his career, he had thousands of followers. Akiba wrote a book entitled, Yetzirah, which is believed to be ascribed to Abraham, and even to Adam. Yetzirah, was first printed in Paris in 1552 The Ether. Seeing this act brought back the memory, of what I had read of the Conjurer Akiba. Could it possibly be that he had reincarnated? I returned to Cyprus quite often after that, usually for a short weekend.

It was part of that exciting time of the sixty's and seventy's, for the younger generation, seemed to have more fun and freedom in this era. Songwriters then, managed to write some wonderful music, for the ballads of that time encapsulated, such beautiful romantic words. These songs have survived the test of time, I have some poems which inspired the song writers, Robert Browning and Elizabeth Barrett, who were favorites of John Lennon and Yoko Ono. Their music is still played in the 21st century and much loved. I enjoyed the arts too, for at one point, I was privileged to have seen, every theater performance in London.

You were able to buy, much more for your money too, however because of decimalization and price changes, this meant that eventually things changed and people had less money to spend after a while. I personally believe, that this was a way of clawing back money from the public and getting the nation's debt down. Credit cards were just posted through doors, without any one applying for them, usually Access cards.

Successive governments, borrowed to support the NHS. The banks had set in motion, a way of getting people to spend more, the price of fuel, goods and services went up. Today there is more poverty and hardship and housing shortages. People take work on Zero contracts and some even work for just food. I guess that's progress for you, with everything loaded in favor of the rich.

Just as everything, seemed to be going great with work and social life, something was about to change. I could feel it fast approaching, with that uncanny feeling of being uneasy, like the time before a storm, after a perfect summers day.

CHAPTER 25
MY LIFE CHANGES DRAMATICALLY

I arrived back at the flat in Camberwell Green, it was a Thursday, the day when I usually met up with my father, however this time it felt different. I entered the bar at the Hermit's Cave and there was my father, sat in his usual seat by the bar. My father seemed his usual jovial self, I knew somehow, that my father would not be with me for much longer and that we would only meet perhaps once or twice after this meeting before he passed, also I knew that my life was going to change in an unrecognizable way, not because of my father but because of an event beyond my control.

Marcos came into the Hermit's Cave, about thirty minutes after my father arrived, he was laughing and joking with us both and then left saying he would be back later, as he was working on a new design he had to finish.

Marcos explained to my father, that whenever he designed a new dress, jacket or coat, he liked me to wear the first one for him. I only weighed six stone at the time and I was the right size to model them. I suppose less material would have been used, in the first garment. Marcos owned his own dress manufacturing company, he worked all hours, he also explained to my father that he nearly lost his business on the turn of a card, when gambling one night, at the local Cafe in Camberwell Green. My father and I both laughed but Marcos was serious. My father and I left shortly after Marcos and we both went back to the attic flat. We had our usual Thursday meal, before returning for a last drink at the Hermits Cave. My father seemed breathless after leaving the Hermits Cave, I said you must give up smoking, it will help with your breathing, he dismissed this and just waved as he got his bus home.

That night I had just gone to sleep, it must have been about 10.30 p.m. when I awoke with a start. There was someone coming up the stairs, then the door to the bedroom opened. There stood Marcos, I asked him who had let him in the front door. Marcos just proceeded to walk into the room, Marcos said that Alec the landlord had, as he had made a plausible excuse. Before I knew it, he was holding me down and I felt the room spinning round, as he forced himself on me. I felt at that very moment, I had become pregnant, as I had a burning sensation inside of me. Of course I would be held to blame, not Marcos, for when I related what had happened to the landlord, I was told to abort, or give up the flat. When I told my father he said the same word "Abort." No one except Marcos thought, I should keep my child, Marcos said "There's always room for one more child in the world." Marcos was married with six children.

I went to check with the local doctor, to see if my prognosis was right, I was advised to come back in two weeks, which I did and my pregnancy was confirmed. I went home that evening, thinking I want to keep my baby, so I sat on the side of the bed and prayed. "If you really are my God, then help me find a way to keep this baby."

It was difficult for an unmarried mother, to keep their baby at that time. They were more often than not, coerced into giving them up for adoption. Sometimes, if an unmarried mother, had no home or means of support, the baby would automatically be taken, by Social Services for adoption. For it was more often than not, deemed to be always the woman, who had been irresponsible.

I went back to work, after hearing the confirmation of my pregnancy. I had bought a London Evening Standard that lunch time and when I had finished my work, I glanced through the adds section, hoping to find somewhere to live. It was now 6 p.m. and most of the office staff had gone home. I was prompted to look in the adds for relationships. The only add that stood out the most, was the one, which said, Gentleman offers home to young lady. I kept doing a double take and eventually summoned up the courage to ring the number. A gentleman answered, "Hello," he said in a soft Northern accent. "I'm still in my office and have just seen your add." I informed him, in a quiet voice. "Yes" he replied, "I placed the add." "Please listen to what I have to say before you hang up, I'm pregnant by only two weeks but I would like to keep my baby, I was raped by someone I knew, everyone seems to be blaming me though and I want to keep my baby, I don't believe in abortion, you can hang up, I won't be offended and I wouldn't blame you, thank you for listening." "No, no, don't go, please don't hang up." he said "Why would you want to bother with me?" I said in a despondent voice.

"My name's Keith, what's your name?" he asked in a soft gentle voice. "My names Penny," I replied. "Can you meet with me this evening?" Keith asked, this time with a protective tone to his voice. "It's getting on for 7 p.m. now" I said. "That's alright can you get to Weybridge Station?" he asked "I will be there at 7.30 p.m. to 8.30 p.m.

depending on the train connection, will that be alright?" "Yes" he said. "Are you absolutely sure?" I asked, "Don't worry, I'll be there for you, I will wait until you arrive."

I met Keith at 8.30 p.m. and he was so kind, with a good sense of humor, a gentleman in every sense of the word. He managed a small local Supermarket and there was a large modern flat over the top, which had three double bedrooms. Keith was and remained the perfect gentleman, the only down side being, that Keith was twenty seven years older than me. Keith was an attractive man, with thick dark wavy hair that had just started, to have flecks of white growing through, at the sides. That night after relating what my circumstances were and explaining what had happened, the night had gone and so I stayed in one of the spare rooms. When I awoke, Keith had gone down to open up the store. There was a note which said, help yourself to tea or coffee and there's some cereal on the work top, milk is in the fridge, I have gone to open up, I'll be back up shortly.

God, who I always referred to as "The Big Chief," had once again answered my prayers.

I rang the firm and told them that something urgent had cropped up and that I had to take the day off. Keith had the afternoon as a half day, so everything worked out perfectly. I rang Alec the landlord of the attic flat, where I was living in Camberwell Green. I explained that I had found accommodation and would be moving out that afternoon. Alec was astonished, that I had made plans so quickly, for he had only informed me a couple of days before, that I would have to move out, if I wasn't prepared to abort my unborn child. Keith and I got on so well and I carried on working, after moving into Keith's flat above the shop, in November 74.

Cyprus was invaded by the Turks that year and divided in two, with Turks on one side of the Island and Cypriots on the other, I never returned to Cyprus again.

By the Christmas of 74, I had received a poetic card everyday, since Keith and I were together. I still have a lot of this beautiful correspondence from Keith, these cards and letters are like precious jewels to me. It was Christmas Eve, when Keith proposed marriage, I said, "Yes, to this wonderful man."

CHAPTER 26
MY FATHER PASSES AWAY

In the January of 1975, I had word that my father had been taken ill, so I rang my sister Pam, to see if she would go and see what was wrong. Pam was unable to go to see him, at his flat in Greenwich, where my brother, wife and their young child, now resided with my father. Pam was expecting her second child and was not well enough to go and see our father, unfortunately, I was unable to go either. The next phone call was to tell me that my father had passed away, he had died in the ambulance, on the way to the hospital. I rang the Coroner who simply explained, that his death had been caused by a lifetime of heavy drinking, this resulted in heart failure, due to deposits of fat around the heart.

I had to go to the flat in Greenwich the following day, as there was no one capable or willing, to make the funeral arrangements. Whilst I was there, my father's sister Betty turned up, with two of her sons and they were grabbing everything that they could carry, without even asking who it belonged to. They had emptied the bedroom and were about to start on the kitchen. I had to tell them to put down the spin dryer, as it belonged to me. They took no account of the fact that my brother Chris, his wife Liz and their son Jason, were staying in the flat. The only time my aunt Betty spoke, was to say that she and his six brothers, would expect me to cater for them after the funeral. This meant they wanted me to organize the whole affair, including the catering.

Aunt Betty didn't like it, when I explained that the death policy, which was to cover the cost of the funeral expenses, was only for two hundred pounds. This was just enough for the burial and two cars, perhaps a few flowers, however, aunt Betty didn't believe me and accused me of trying to keep some money back. Her next sentence was, that the family would never talk to me again, if you don't cater for them. I asked her, if they were prepared, to put their hands in their pockets and pay for this so called party, after the funeral. "You surely, don't expect us to pay for it," was the reply. I said, "If you or any of the family, choose to never talk to me again, there certainly would be no change there, as they have never spoken to me before, have they?" During the time that all the belongings were being lifted out, of my father's flat in Greenwich, there was no word of sympathy or help offered towards me, not even one card was given, from any of his brothers or his sister.

When the day of the funeral came, Keith and I drove from Weybridge, to Shooters Hill Cemetery. My sister Pam was unable to attend the funeral, for as I previously mentioned, Pam was expecting her second child, so there was only my brother Chris and his wife Liz in the Limo, following the Hearse. Keith and I arrived at the chapel, in our own car. My father's family did not inform me, as to whether they would be attending or not.

Keith parked our car and I went into the little church, which was situated in the grounds of Shooters Hill Cemetery. My brother Chris and his wife Liz, didn't even bother to look round. Half way through the service, there was some noise at the back of the church and my aunt Betty together with some of my father's brothers turned up, rather late for the ceremony. When the service was over, I followed my father's coffin, towards the graveside and It was at this point that my father appeared beside me and he smiled. Some how, he had managed to make me feel that he was supporting me, throughout this awful experience.

My father's family, together with Chris and Liz, stood the other side of the grave, whilst I stood alone, next to the Spirit form of my father.

I placed a single red rose into the grave, and said goodbye to the Spirit of my father, having told him to go into the light. I turned and started to walk up the hill, towards our car, when suddenly a very overweight man, came running up the hill behind me. He introduced himself as Abe, my father's eldest brother. He gasped and said, "I wanted to say I'm sorry, for the way you were treated." I just turned to face him, looking him straight in the eyes, "It's too late now, I don't even know any of you, but nevertheless, thank you." I carried on up the grassy hill, towards where Keith was waiting by the car. It was such a relief, to be closing the door, on this episode of my life and all the bad memories, that were so prevalent throughout my childhood.

CHAPTER 27
I GO FORWARD WITH MY LIFE WITH KEITH

Keith and I went back to the flat in Addlestone near Weybridge and for once in my life, I felt relaxed and at home. I carried on working in London, until a few weeks before my baby, was due to be born.

Keith would drop me off at the Station every morning, with a copy of the Guardian to read on the train, for he was such a thoughtful and caring person. When I returned, Keith would be waiting, to collect me from the Station every evening, having cooked dinner for us before leaving. He had done all this for me, after having had to manage the small Super Market all day. Keith had a wonderful sense of humor and always managed to make me laugh, I was so blessed that the Big Chief had brought Keith into my life. "Never under estimate the power of prayer, to bring an Angel into your life."

Keith had asked me to marry him, the first Christmas after we had met and continued to write to me every day, either a card or a letter, in which he wrote of his love for me, in such an endearing way. As mentioned previously, I still have these beautiful cards and letters to this very day, for those beautiful words, are and always will, remain like jewels of the soul. Keith and I were married, in the first week, of July 1975.

One night I had retired to bed early, I had one of the double rooms, Keith was in another, as he did not want to disturb me, for at this time, I was such a light sleeper. I awoke to see smoke around the bed, I could hear Keith's little black cat, meowing in the background. Feeling my baby stretch out inside me, I arose and went into the lounge where the light was on, I thought that Keith must have retired to bed and left the light on. I could not see the cat anywhere and felt that she must have climbed out of the kitchen window that Keith always left open for her.

The doorbell rang and I looked at the clock, it was now 11 p.m. as I opened the front door. There stood my father in the blue suit that I had bought for him, only weeks before he had passed away. My mind did not register straightaway that he had died, I just thought that he had come for a visit. He came into the lounge, sat down in the armchair opposite me. "I want you to clear up something for me," my father said. "Just a moment, I will go and make us a milky drink first," I told him. The kitchen was just off the lounge and this I did and went on back through to the lounge, placing the drinks on the coffee table. We spoke for a short time and my father never touched his drink, instead after speaking, he just said that he had to go, as it was getting late. As it was such a brief visit, I concluded that he had a taxi waiting. My father made no attempt to give me a hug before he left, I thought that he must just be tired, for I still had not awoken to the fact that he had died. After he had left, I put the cups to soak in the kitchen and went back to bed.

When I awoke, Keith had already gone down to open up the shop. I washed and dressed and on going through to the kitchen, I could see the two cups were still there. I turned to see the kitchen window still open and Keith's little black cat came bounding in, through the open window. The cat followed me to the bathroom, she was anxious and unsettled. I turned and felt she was trying to tell me, that what I had witnessed, she had too, regarding my father's visit last night.

I looked at the bath, the cat jumped into the bath and wet, when I looked at the sink, the cat jumped into the sink and wet. Walking through to one of the double bedrooms, the cat followed me, jumped onto the middle of the bed, and wet. Something strange had been witnessed by both of us, the night before and we were both feeling unsettled. I rang down to the shop and asked Keith, if he had time to come up, as the cat was acting strange. This he did and when Keith walked into the flat, he could see that the cat was acting strange. "Keith, the cat is following me all over the flat, she jumps in front of me and wherever I look she wets."

Of course he found this statement incredible, so I demonstrated what was going on, by asking him to follow me into the bathroom, this he did. Keith, I am going to look at the bath first, this I did and the cat jumped into the bath and wet. Now I'm going to look into the sink, this I did and the cat wet in the sink. Keith I am going to go into the bedroom, he followed and the cat shot passed us both, jumped into the middle of the bed and wet. By this time Keith had become angry at the antics of his cat, so he picked her up and put her outside, shutting the kitchen window.

Fight Back To Eternity

Keith returned to work and I carried on with the housework, cleaning and washing the bedding, I remember the smell of OMO, which made me feel nausea's. I hoped that the little black cat, after being chastised by Keith, had managed to pull herself together.

The little black cat had somehow, tried to communicate to me, the fact that she too had seen my father visit, the night before, in his Spirit form. Keith came back up, after closing the shop at lunchtime, he relented and let the cat back in. We managed to make light of the morning's event, so after lunch Keith returned to the shop downstairs. I washed up and sat down to watch the tennis on the TV, however something stranger, was about to unfold that afternoon. The July of 1975 was hot and so was I, perspiring profusely, as my baby was due any time soon. I had the kitchen window and front door open and had just settled to watch the tennis, when I could hear the meow, of the little black cat at my feet. I looked down and she had put an entire nest of baby birds at my feet. I rang down to the shop and yet again a bewildered Keith, had to deal with another incident regarding his cat. He had only just returned to the shop, when yet another incident unfolded, with the little black cat. She was trying to please me, as a short time after this, she came into the flat and dropped a nest of baby mice at my feet. Yet again Keith had to leave the shop to dispose of another nest, this one being full of mice. After closing the shop, we had a little talk, about the events that had unfolded. I explained about seeing my father the night before but I don't think Keith believed me. We had our dinner and Keith's African gray parrot, which I had been trying to get to talk, suddenly started to do so. The parrot had not uttered a word since Keith had bought it some years ago. I had placed the parrot cage, just behind the door in the lounge, not letting the parrot see anything for some weeks. I just allowed the parrot, who was called Tom, to hear me saying, "Tom," every now and then. The parrot once it started talking, would talk incessantly, mimicking everything. It sung every advert on the television and we had to cover Tom up, every now and then, to get some peace and quiet. The following day, we thought that the episode with the little black cat, had finally ended, however we were sadly mistaken.

Following on after the incident with the baby bird's nest and also that of the baby mice, being put at my feet, the little black cat brought our neighbor's cat, through the kitchen window. They charged around the lounge, like a couple of energetic toddlers, knocking everything over, including that which was remaining on the mantelpiece. When Keith came up from the shop for lunch, the lounge looked like a war zone, this went on for a couple of days, as did the wetting in front of me.

Keith and I were having lunch one Wednesday, having planned on going out, for the afternoon. We liked to go and visit the auctions, as we often did on a Wednesday, with this now being Keith's day off. We were sitting there, when the little black cat, brought her partner in crime, our neighbor's cat with her, through the partly open kitchen window, Keith got up quickly and rushed into the kitchen. The little black cat escaped through the kitchen window, leaving the neighbor's tabby trapped by Keith, in the kitchen. Keith locked the kitchen door and without me knowing, drowned the neighbor's cat. I did not find out, what Keith had done with the neighbor's cat, until a couple of days later. Our neighbors were calling for their cat, they knocked on our door and said, "We're trying to trace the cat, have you seen her?" Keith and I were having tea that Sunday afternoon and no sooner had they gone, than Keith admitted that they wouldn't find the cat, as he had buried it in the woods, I thought that Keith had been cleaning the kitchen floor, because the cats had knocked the kettle over, the day before. Thinking that they must have made another mess, when he had shut me out of the kitchen, not realizing

Fight Back To Eternity

he was drowning the neighbor's cat. As the days went by, Keith's little black cat, continued to knock the ornaments off the mantelpiece and wet, so Keith made the difficult decision, to have the little black cat put down.

By the end of July, my son was due to be born and Keith was present at the birth of my son. As there were too few midwives, Keith was left alone with me, whilst our son was being born. Keith practically had to deliver him, strangely I felt no labor pains, just a back ache, as I was born without a pelvic muscle. The head was delivered, when the midwife came in, unfortunately she had to cut me, and I had to have extensive stitches, inside and out, which caused complications. Episiotomies were the norm at this particular time, as it was practiced, as part of the qualification for midwifery. There was also a rather strange auxiliary nurse, in charge of the ward at this time. As mothers were made to stay in bed for ten days in 1975, this auxiliary nurse got over excited, if you even got out of bed to comb your hair. So most mothers would wind her up, on a daily basis, as this proved to be a source of amusement. You were only allowed to feed your baby by the clock too, with all babies taken back to the nursery after feeding. You were not allowed to get up and feed them during the night either. The day finally came, for Keith and I, to take our beautiful son home. As I had informed Keith about the auxiliary nurse, who was more than strange, to say the least, he watched over our baby Tony like a hawk, as she insisted on carrying him to the car and we breathed a sigh of relief, to be away from the hospital. Ten days was such a long time, to have to spend in hospital after the birth, this being the normal practice at that time, there was little we could do.

After bringing Tony home, early the following morning, we had a visit from the district midwife, to see how the baby was doing, and how we were coping with our new baby. I remember that this particular morning was hot and my son was a restless baby. Keith and I had to place the carrycot in the middle of the bed. We had to surround the carrycot with cushions, as our son would kick himself out of the carrycot. Keith's mother came over to stay with us from Canada, Jacques was also a French Canadian name. Keith's brother Mark, had a ship building business in Canada and with his wife Kate, they also ran their own finance company. Keith and his brother were born in Beeston, both being born in the Derbyshire area, however Mark had emigrated to Canada. Keith and Mark, both had aunts and uncles in Australia too. I understand, they were among the ten pound poms, who emigrated to Australia, when they were children with their parents, so they spent a part of their childhood in Australia, before finally returning to England, when they were still small children. So they had relatives in Queensland Australia, where their aunt had a banana plantation, having married a Colonial Lord.

Life settled into a routine over the next few weeks, after his mother Lesley had gone back to Canada, to stay with his brother. After a short stay in Canada, Lesley wrote to say that she was traveling onto Queensland, to see her sister. Shortly after Keith's mother Lesley had gone abroad, he had decided to find a house for us, as he felt our son Tony, would need a garden to play in. Keith applied to manage a Supermarket, on a new housing estate, in Northampton with a large garden, surrounding the house. So before our son Tony was a month old, we moved to Northampton. The house was a large and spacious newly built property, with a manageable garden. It was heated with warm air heating, which was a new form of heating in the seventies. The summer of 1975, was one of the hottest and this was followed, by an even hotter year in 1976. Keith and I managed to get some second hand furniture, to fill the house and we had olive green carpet fitted throughout. We bought a second hand washing machine after a while, before then, it would take me three hours a day, to keep the washing down. I was boiling nappies and washing bed linen and clothes all by hand, as well as looking after a new baby and cooking and cleaning. I did not realize that being on my feet for such long hours, after the problems of child birth, would cause me to have to go in for major surgery. This being to sort out the physical problems, after the birth of our son. Fortunately Keith's mother, offered to come back from Australia, to look after things, whilst I was hospitalized. Keith insisted that I had the operation privately, as it had been such a bodged job before. Unfortunately he had to sell our much loved parrot Tom, to pay for the operation. Shortly after the operation in November 76 and after such a hot summer, we then had a very cold winter, with heavy snow.

Keith's mother had gone to Canada to stay with his brother Mark and his wife Kate and life seemed to settle into a steady routine once more. Once our son Tony was walking at nine months old, he was even more active, Tony would bounce himself out of his cot, onto the padded ottoman and climb down, to try and get over the gate in his room. Keith had to install another gate across the stairs, so that we could catch him, before he managed to climb over, the second gate. As Tony was so hyperactive, Keith and I got very little sleep. Tony would sleep for four hours at the most, I didn't realize at the time that Tony was made hyperactive, by orange juice that contained E additives.

CHAPTER 28
HEARTACHE ONCE MORE

After the lovely summer, there followed a bad winter, the snow continued for some weeks and everywhere was icy. On one of these mornings, my Clairvoyance kicked in. My Heavenly Parents were talking, "Tell Keith not to use the front door, when he goes out to work this morning." Yes, it was my Spiritual Parents again, I had not heard from them for some time, so I knew it must be serious. Keith was ready to go out. I said "Keith whatever you do, don't go out the front door to work." Keith looked at me in disbelief, "Whatever for?" He asked. "Just don't ask, please go out the back gate across the grass, it's far too icy on the front path," I pleaded with him. However he took no notice, telling me not to be so silly and that he would be perfectly fine. He opened the front door and once on the front path, slipped and fell backwards with a heavy thud. Keith hit the back of his neck, on the metal strip across the door step, knocking himself unconscious, and I found him laying prostrate, on the icy path. I wondered how I was going to get him back inside, for Keith was a tall and well built man. I supported his neck, I don't know how I managed it, but somehow I did, to gradually and carefully get him back inside into the hall. I closed the door against the cold icy blast, it had started to snow heavily, as I closed the front door. I managed, once he had gained consciousness, to ease Keith into an armchair. Fortunately, Keith had given his assistant manageress Carole, a set of keys to open the store, in case the weather had continued to deteriorate. Carole lived over the news agents, opposite the Supermarket. I rang Carole at the Supermarket and explained that Keith had fallen and had slipped on the icy path, when going out the front door. I explained that the blow he took, on the back of his neck, had knocked him unconscious. Keith had told me to say that he would give her a call, once he had recovered from the shock.

I gave Keith some brandy in warm water to sip, when Keith had recovered enough by lunchtime, he insisted on going into work. This time he listened and walked across the grass, without any further harm. However the blow to the back of the neck, though it left bruising, whilst not resulting in any broken bones, nevertheless manifested into something else, which was to be much more serious.

A few weeks after the accident, Keith had difficulty in swallowing and as he was not one to go and visit a GP, I had to really insist on this occasion. Keith finally gave in and agreed to see his GP, the doctor insisted that Keith went for a biopsy. The result came back, with Cancer of the Esophagus, Keith and I were both devastated. Keith explained that he may have been in contact with radiation, in his career in the Royal Marines. Keith was on the Nuclear Submarines and I guess this may have somehow, contributed towards the Cancer which lay dormant, until the blow on the back of the neck, when he had fallen on the icy path.

Tony was still a baby, Keith was heart broken that he might not be there to see him grow up. It was made even more bizarre, because

Keith had just gone the previous week, for a job interview at the co-op. This was for the undertakers which seemed unbelievable, given his current health situation, terminal Cancer. Keith had wanted a change of career and being the kind considerate person he was, this job, strange as it may seem, would have suited his personality, for Keith was always calm under difficult circumstances.

Keith telephoned his mother, who was staying with his brother Mark and wife Kate. Lesley, Keith's mother, agreed to take the next flight back to the UK. We both went through that week in a kind of surreal daydream. The hospital Surgeon had advised, that there was a slim chance, he might be able to remove the cancer, so an appointment was made for surgery. This was in the January, following the December diagnosis. Unfortunately there was nothing they could do and I lost Keith, just eight days after surgery. I went home on my own, devastated and in total utter shock, how on earth was I going to break the news to Keith's mother Lesley, I thought to myself. I arrived back at the house and found my mother in law sitting on the stairs. I guess she knew, even before I said anything, as Lesley must have seen that I was looking very white faced, I broke the news and we both cried together, comforting each other. We decided to bath Tony and give him his tea early, so that we could put him to bed. Lesley and I then retired to bed early that night, we were both tired and mentally exhausted, with the shock of it all.

Tony my baby son, was awake by 5 a.m. and Keith's mother was up early too, neither of us having slept at all. We didn't feel like eating, so we just looked after Tony between us and then I had to contact the firm, where Keith worked, to say that he had passed away. I then had to contact the Co-op funeral service, to arrange Keith's funeral and he was buried that same week, my mother in law stayed, until after the funeral before returning to Canada. Lesley was heart broken too and did not attend the funeral but remained at home, to take care of Tony. There was only a representative from Keith's firm, along with myself at the graveside. I had a letter not long after Keith had died, to say that his mother had passed away too, shortly after returning to her sister's in Australia. Lesley had stopped taking her heart medication, having lost the will to live. My sister in law wrote to me, to break the sad news, which came as yet another shock. Kate went on to say in the letter, that she would welcome some help, in the company business. I was told if I wanted to emigrate to Canada with Tony, I would be made welcome, however I decided to stay in the UK.

Not long after the funeral, Keith appeared, he was standing washing his hands at the sink, he had said that if he passed on, he would come back and give me a sign, that he was all right. By coming home, this was his way of letting me know. I had to tell him to go into the light. "Keith you know I love you, much more than words can say but you cannot stay, you must go into the light." He smiled and was gone. A gentleman made the journey from the War Office in London, he came in and sat himself down. I made him a cup of tea and he proceeded to tell me that I was entitled to a War Pension because of Keith's service. He confirmed what Keith had told me, in that when his ship was torpedoed, there were just three of them, who initially survived in a life boat. Keith and one other, after three days in the open lifeboat, were the only two survivors left. Many years into the future, I would do a reading on a train journey for Keith's co survivor, this involved giving a message to his daughter. However I digress, the gentleman from the War Office said, that because I was a lot younger than Keith, he would only be offering me 5p a week. I said, "What about the fact that Keith and I have a young son?" He replied that it was based on my ability to work. I asked him, "Why did you bother to come, all the way from the War Office in London, you could have just put a letter in the post." then added, "If that's all Keith was worth to the War Office, that he had better keep the 5p a week." I then showed him out. After the gentleman from the War Office had gone, I read the letter which had arrived that same day, from Keith's sister in law Kate, to see if I would change my mind, as Kate had asked, if I would like to go out to Canada,

CHAPTER 29
I TRY TO MOVE FORWARD WITH MY LIFE

Not long after Keith's passing, two Mormon missionaries knocked on the door, one was called Elder Former but I cannot recall the name of the other. Elder Former was a tall young man with a soft American accent. I beheld a beautiful light, which shone all around him and I could see a wonderful presence with him too. After several visits, I became baptized and I was known as Sister Jacques, this being my first married name. I found a local job, that had a nursery facility and took Tony to work with me. A neighbor would drive Tony and I to Church's Shoe Company each morning and collect and bring us home every evening. It was also whilst working at the Shoe Company, that I was buying and selling old cars, purchased from auction. I would pay an elderly gentleman £50 per car, for doing them up and I would then sell them on privately. Jeff, whilst being a hotel porter, was also a brilliant mechanic and was glad of the extra money, to buy his whiskey. I was determined to get off the estate, where I found my self on my own with Tony, after Keith's demise from Cancer.

Whilst working at Church's shoe company, an elderly foreman, a Mr Jackson, said that Des O'Connor, once worked there, saying that he had gone on to become a Red Coat. Whether this was true or otherwise, I could only take his word for it. Des O'Connor is a wonderful singer and comedian and well loved by most people. I was also led to believe that in fun, he had danced on the switchboard.

I enjoyed the work in the stock room, for it was well heated and clean work and most importantly, I could also see and wave at my little son Tony, whilst he was playing in the playground, near the nursery below. Later I saved enough money to put him in a private school, Park Side Academy and Tony looked very smart in his purple blazer.

The Christmas after Keith's passing, I wanted to be away from the house, So with a friend, who was also a single parent, we spent that Christmas at a hotel, Father Christmas arrived by helicopter that year. As I was working hard, I managed to get a small deposit on a terraced house, which was just a short distance from Church's Shoe Company, also it was nearer the Church of Jesus Christ of Later Day Saints, also known as (LDS). I was still looking for answers, regarding my Spiritual gifts and I was hoping to find the answers, through religion.

I left Church's Shoe Company, not long after moving from the housing estate house, that I shared with Keith in Northampton. At that time I had two cleaning jobs, a catering job at the weekend and a 9 a.m. to 5 p.m. job during the week, with the Royal Insurance, as an Audio typist, whilst Tony was at a private school. My other job after leaving the Royal Insurance, was as a receptionist, typist telex operator, at the Saxon Inn Market Square, Northampton.

As time went by, I eventually met and married again, he was a white South African chef called Louie, who worked at another of the hotels. We sold up and had enough to go and make the journey to his family, in South Africa. However after not having been married very long, I found that the apartheid situation in South Africa, was to get in the way of our marriage.

I remember taking a train to Durban one day, with my young son Tony. There was a smart young man in a cream business suit, who started to make conversation with Tony and I. The train guard came into the carriage and asked to see the tickets. The guard then turned to the young man and said to him, "Net Blacks" which means that you can't sit in a white carriage. The young man who was neither black or white replied. "I was told to come here, as I am not black." "Net Blacks." the guard replied once more. With that he stopped the train and bodily threw this young man, from the train in the middle of nowhere. Just before going to the railway station to board a train for Durban, there was another incident. I had gone into a shop to purchase some food and cakes for the day out. A small child, around my son's age, tugged at my sleeve and asked, if I would buy him a cake? He asked politely, saying he was very hungry, I remembered the time in my own childhood, when I too was hungry, so I gladly bought him a cake. The only thing is, I wish I hadn't, because a South African security guard was watching. I said that I had willingly given the cake, as the boy was the same age as my own son. The guard replied, "Blacks are not allowed to approach Whites." The child who was held by a security guard broke free, and ran for his life. The child's only crime, was being brave enough through hunger, to ask me to buy him a cake. The Security Guard ran after him, he wanted to harm the child. I had not realized that I had put this poor child, in such danger. I returned to the UK with my son and had to start again, for Louie, who was also sympathetic, towards fellow human beings, who just happened to be black, had disappeared and when I tried the legal route to try and trace him, I found every door firmly shut, in respect of all of my inquiries. Eventually I divorced in his absence, after Tony and I had returned to the UK and I settled in the Medway Towns.

I had left my car, in what I thought were my sister's trusting hands. Hopefully my twin might still have my car and I was praying, that this would be the case, as my car once sold, would have given my son Tony and I, enough money to get settled again. When I asked for my car, Pam informed me that she had sold it, as she was in need of the money at the time. However as I was still in need of a place to live, with my young son Tony, Pam suggested that I go and see a friend of hers, on the Isle of Sheppey, called Gordon. He had a fabricating business and was in need of a secretary and someone to do the book keeping and typing, this I was told, would have the offer of a flat also. I looked at this offer, as a gift from heaven and I went along to see Gordon and he seemed a very nice person and after a short interview, I took the job. I felt that this was an ideal situation, to get started once more, there was a good Junior school, within walking distance of the flat too. The flat was peaceful, though sparsely furnished, with just the one double bed. The Swale house as it was called, overlooked the Causeway in Queenborough, there were beautiful sunsets over the water on fine days. This flat gave my son Tony and I a place to be happy in, whilst healing from past traumas.

I met with the local Vicar and his wife the March's and we soon became friends. Jean March helped, with finding my son Tony and I some clothes, also furniture for the flat, for I had to leave my belonging's in Cape Town. My young son Tony and I were happy though, I was content, even though we had very little in the way of material things.

Tony by now aged five, was attending the local school in Queenborough, on the Isle of Sheppey. He had settled in well, also he had made some new friends, as the people in Queenborough were very friendly. All was well for a while, but sometimes, when things go so well and you are happy, you just know that it could all change, in the blink of an eye and whilst I was working in the office, it did. Gordon was having a problem getting a big client, to pay for the work, he had carried out for them, the Company was based on the Island. Thirty thousand pounds was a lot of money, back in the late seventy's, for a small company to lose and it was enough to put Gordon out of business, it only took months, before Gordon in fact was.

Gordon and my sister Pam, were friends with another businessman called Martin, whose family wanted a housekeeper, also someone to help out in the business. A similar job opportunity, work and accommodation had presented itself. Once again I had accommodation and a small wage amounting to just fifteen pounds a week, this I was told to put towards the house keeping, by Martin's mother. Martin's father paid for a Bungalow in Upchurch and Tony and I settled in, I guess Martin's family wanted him to have a place of his own, at the age of thirty three.

Martin was a very difficult person at times, especially when he had been drinking and I found myself in a situation, following one of his drunken nights out and once again became pregnant, this time with a little girl. The reader might wonder, why my clairvoyance let me down, however when you are down and out and consumed by utter devastation, it makes it all the more harder, to tune in. Where were my Heavenly Parents, the reader may inquire? I am of the firm belief, that all these trials and tribulations, were meant to make me a stronger person. I would be able to, in the future, more easily link in to all the people, that I would come into contact with, requesting my help, in so many diverse situations. You cannot assist, advise or help anyone, unless you have been through, the same many complex situations, that they are going through, if you have not already experienced them, fully yourself. How can you therefore understand others, who are going through similar circumstances. None of us are perfect, if we only have the truth of mind, to own up and admit it, with two old sayings springing to mind, "There but for the grace of God, go I" and, "People in glass houses, should not throw stones".

At this time, I became friends with my neighbor, who had just had a baby girl, only weeks before, I became pregnant. I wanted to keep my weight down after the birth, so my neighbor recommended, that I go on the diet plan that she had used. After my neighbor had given me the address of her supplier, I went along to a lady in Rochester, who had a stock of this diet food. I had been expected and was shown into the lounge. A lady called Anne, was sat on the sofa, sorting through this stock of diet meals. Looking at Anne, I could see the same beautiful light, that I had seen around Elder Former, all those years ago in Northampton, it was so beautiful this light. My first words to Anne were, "You're a Mormon!" Anne looked at me in astonishment, "How could you possible know that, we have never met before." I replied. "I just know these things." I could sense that Anne, was going through a difficult time, with her husband too. Anne was married to an alcoholic, as yet though, we didn't really know the full extent of the situations, that we were both living through. Anne and I became very supportive to each other, and good friends for decades to come. Over the years we supported and helped each other, in so many ways. Anne also would talk to me over the phone, realizing that I was becoming more and more traumatized, by the day.

Martin and I did marry, after our daughter was born, but eventually I had to take the advice of a solicitor, as it was becoming increasingly traumatic, on a daily basis, for it wasn't easy dealing with his alcoholic behavior. However this experience was to prove invaluable, in helping others, who were going through a traumatic time, within their marriage or partnerships. In the future I would be helping women and men, who were suffering from the bizarre behavior, caused by those who are alcoholic. I further didn't realize that my schooling as a Medium, included all the traumas of life, with so much crammed into one lifetime. I guess in short, without realizing these experiences were the grounding, of what I was destined to become, for I was still seeking the answers through religion. Anne was helping me over the phone, telling me about the LDS venues and events and this helped me, to have some sense of normality.

One lunchtime, my sister Pam just dropped in, with an elderly gentleman, who she introduced to me as Len Hull. Evidently, he was smitten with my sister Pam and they told me, that they were going for a trip to Italy together. Len was the father of Rod Hull, who was made famous by the antics of Emu his puppet. Rod Hull would be remembered, for his puppet's attack on Michael Parkinson, during one of his shows. Len and I stayed friends for some time, even after the difficult birth of my daughter who was premature. I didn't tell, either Len or my sister, what a difficult life I had at the time. Len lived on a static mobile home park in Yalding, Kent and I asked Len, why he did not live in a house. "I prefer to live here." he simply said, because he was happy where he was. Unfortunately this site was often flooded, Len made miniature antique chairs as a hobby and he told me that his son Rod, had married Jack Hylton's daughter Cher. Jack Hylton was a very famous bandleader of the 1920s and 1940s. I personally believe that he was one of the great bandleaders of all time. Jack Hylton must go down in musical history as being world class for his dance and band music. Len would often chat to me, about his son Rod and daughter in law Cher. He would be chatting away, whilst making these intricate little chairs, on his miniature lathe. Len even said that Rod and Rolf Harris were good friends, but I can only take his word for it. He would often chat regarding Jim Breedon, who was the owner of the site that he lived on. I believe that his hobby making antique miniature chairs, must have kept him occupied, when trapped by flooding every winter.

Shortly after this, I went into hospital and had my premature baby girl, who I named Sophia. Previously I had asked Martin, if he would buy a pram and a cot, with his reply being, why should I bother to waste my money, adding, I don't want you to even bring it home, if it's not a boy.

My sister Pam, had kept her daughters baby clothes, which she passed on to me, so at least I had some clothes for her. I managed to buy a second hand carry cot for £2.00 and a second hand cot, also for £2.00. I cleaned the carrycot and painted the old cot, to make it look like new. Due to never being able to relax, whilst being married to Martin, the placenta had stopped feeding my baby girl. Sophia only weighed 4lb. 11oz when born by caesarean and I only came to hold my baby daughter, three days later. It was explained to me, that whilst they were performing the Caesarean, they had cut through one of the arteries and I was given, a five pint blood transfusion. A nurse sat on my bed and said, " I shouldn't tell you this but felt you should know what happened." The nurse then kindly told me, this was why I had been in bed for three days, with a high temperature. Sophia had to stay in hospital for a lot longer, due to a heart murmur and because of the domestic complications. Even though I had been through so much, there was no kindness shown from Martin, or his sister Doreen, when they had visited. One of the comments I received from Doreen was, "You have had one, now you can have another one and next time hopefully, it will be a boy." The comment from my husband was, "You needn't think, that you can just sit around, when you get home, there's plenty of work for you to do." I was exhausted after the Caesarean and in the Elizabeth ward, I kept drifting in and out of consciousness. I had just opened my eyes and could see there was an English lady in the bed opposite. Her husband who was visiting, to look at his new born son, was shouting at his wife who was crying. "What are you so upset about, why are you crying?" Adding whilst he gazed into the crib at his son. "I can't see anything wrong with him, he looks alright to me." his wife still sobbing, said he.. he's a Mongol baby." "That's it, you can get dressed right now, we're going out of here now and you are not bringing that thing home." They both left together, leaving their beautiful new born son still laying in his crib. The following day in the same bed that the English lady had occupied, there was another lady looking into the crib beside her bed crying, she was an Indian lady, who was already dressed to leave, and return home. Her husband came in and was very angry with her. He never glanced into the crib, just pushed his wife, who was sobbing, out the door and was still shouting and cursing at her, the staff tried to stop them but they just left. They did not take the baby girl with them, or even give a backward glance. It was as if they had just left this beautiful baby girl, to whatever fate held for her. The nurse came across to me and explained that some Indian families, dread the birth of a baby girl. "Some of these little girls, are murdered just for being born female." The nurse was full of apologies, as this was the second time in just two days that I had witnessed the abandonment of two little infants. One being a Mongol boy, and the other a little Indian girl, both these little infants, were beautiful to look at. They both had a beautiful gold light around them, they must have been very special high realm Spirits, destined for great things. When the nurse returned from the nursery, where she had just placed the little new born girl, she came across to me and said that the babies would be fed in their cribs, as they were not allowed to pick them up. I found this incredible that an abandoned infant would be denied contact whilst being fed, if you fed a puppy you would give some contact. "Indian girls, are treated differently to boys, and only the birth of a boy, would be celebrated in most cases." the Nurse explained. So in the May of 1983, there in the nursery at All Saints Hospital in Chatham, Kent, lay two beautiful unwanted babies, one boy and one girl. Was all that I had witnessed in the Elizabeth ward, a lesson that would enhance my empathy towards others? I had not been valued myself, by my family, for as a child I was treated, like a non entity, at this point my Heavenly Parents informed me, that I would be reading for many people in the future, who were of the Indian culture.

It had been three days of drifting in and out of consciousness and I had not seen my baby and no one had informed me that I too, had given birth to a baby girl. A Nurse approached me, and I had to inquire about my baby, who was born by Caesarian. The nurse looked astonished, that no one had told me that I had given birth to a baby girl, she explained that my baby girl, was in an incubator and was in the special care unit. The nurse had a Polaroid camera and offered to take a photo of my baby girl, she later handed me the photo and asked, if I wanted to give her a name. I said yes, I named her Sophia Elizabeth. Elizabeth after the ward, in which the two little infants, had been rejected by their parents. I only hoped that this would not happen to me, as I had given birth to a baby girl, for Martin's words, kept replaying in my mind, "If it's not a boy, don't bother to bring it home."

Whilst I was in hospital, Martin had dug the back garden up, so consequently, when the two dogs went to the back garden and relieved themselves, they would trail mud, right the way through the bungalow.

I had to return home on my own, as Sophia still had to stay in special care. Martin had left for work, the phone rang just as I walked into the front door, expecting it to be Martin. The phone call was from Martin's mother, she did not ask me how I was keeping, instead just told me that she had sent her cleaner over, to clean the bungalow. I said, "That was very thoughtful, thank you." In the very next sentence, Martin's mother blamed me for the mess, which her son had created. "You filthy cow, now keep it that way." were her last words before slamming the phone down.

Martin had informed the hospital, that he would be passing the baby over to his eldest sister Doreen, who was a ex nurse, as the baby was premature, he had also stated that I would not be capable of bringing Sophia up. When the visiting nursing inspector arrived at the bungalow, Martin made the same statement to her. My son Tony was standing next to me, "Who raised this little boy?" she said looking straight into Martin's eyes. After appraising my eight year old son Tony, the nursing inspector repeated the same question. "Who raised this little boy?." "She did." Martin replied. "Do you mean your wife raised him alone?" queried the nurse, "Yes" said Martin, red faced and angry, that he was not about to get his own way. "Well I see nothing wrong, in the way your wife has raised her son, I will keep the baby in hospital for a while, in order to give your wife time to recover from the Caesarian." Martin walked through to the garden with the dogs. The nursing inspector then took me to one side, and said, "It's quite common for wealthy families, to push the mother to one side, and take over the baby." Adding, "Please try and get yourself alternative accommodation and if you should need more time, let me know."

As much as I tried to break free from the situation, it proved an impossibility. When they checked my statements with Martin he said, that there was nothing wrong. I lived in an expensive bungalow and drove an expensive car, adding I was well taken care of. Of course, coming from a wealthy family in the Medway Towns, they believed him. Martin had planned, to give our daughter away, to his eldest sister Doreen, he had refused to buy anything for the baby, possible because this had all been planed, prior to my giving birth to our daughter.

Martin being an alcoholic, would spend £20 a night on drink, plus he would buy panatella cigars. Martin's self indulgence meant that his only daughter, would have to rely on charity, whatever others were kind enough to give, regarding baby clothes, toys or books.

The landlord of a local pub, near Upchurch, would loan him a bottle of brandy or whiskey to take home and he would replace it, when he went there on his next visit. Quite often, Martin would not know where, or indeed what, he had used as a toilet, when he was so drunk, at times it had been on baby clothes, books or toys.

Martin would constantly complain about me to his parents, one example being, that I was spending an extra penny, on the purchase of gold top milk, for our daughter Sophia. Martin's behavior was bazaar, he would complain that I had not cut open the pump dispenser, to use the last remnants of toothpaste. So because of this, he would state, I was wasting his money. Another example being that I had put two tea bags in the tea pot to make him a cup of tea. This was all meant to cause an argument and make my life unbearable. He once snatched, a small jar of baby food from me, throwing the jar against the wall. "You are poisoning the baby," he said as it hit the wall, this was the unreasonable behavior of an alcoholic.

Before our daughter Sophia was a year old, we were invited for a week, to his eldest sister in Plymouth, supposedly to give me a break, however this proved to be a lot more sinister. Whilst there, she took over looking after Sophia, as I was expected to keep occupied, by doing all the housework and cooking. I was standing on the stairs after just cleaning the bedrooms, which were thickly stained with nicotine, when I overheard Doreen, on the phone to Martin's mother. My mother in law asked, "Is she going to leave the baby with you?" with the reply being, "I haven't told her yet." I was furious. "What on earth are you talking about, I came with two children and I'm leaving with two children and right now, otherwise I will be calling the police." Martin didn't know what to do, for they had planned it all between them, they assumed, that I had no rights whatsoever, Doreen tried to make out, it was to give me a rest. I took Sophia from her and Tony put our things in the car, Martin was angry and silent all the way home. Once we were all back at the bungalow in Upchurch, I went inside with the two children and Martin stormed out the front door, to go drinking.

Martin's eldest sister Doreen rang, just after he had gone out, I picked up the phone, before I could say anything, Doreen went on to say, that she felt as though she was on a treadmill. Thinking she was talking figuratively at first, I was about to say, perhaps it is you that needs to take a break. You should put all thoughts of ever looking after my children out of your mind. These are my children, just concentrate on looking after your own husband, and your children. However before I could get these statements out, Doreen stated, "I have snakes in my head, and also poison hooks in my head." I replied, "Doreen you need help, please go and see your doctor first thing in the morning." "Can I ring you again?" Doreen asked. "Of course, if you feel I can help you in anyway, please let me know." I was trying to sound as sympathetic as possible having realized how ill, Doreen really was

I was not long after this conversation with Doreen, that she was sectioned under the mental health act. Doreen had shut the family dog in the cupboard, and set fire to her house, leaving the house to burn, with her husband and children remaining asleep inside. Doreen had then calmly vacated the burning house. The fire had started to take hold, whilst her husband and children were still sleeping, it was only the sound of the dog frantically barking, that woke the family, the dog had saved their lives.

Martin's father put a million pounds, towards the cost of looking after Doreen. This was to insure that his eldest daughter Doreen, was to get the best of supervised care, for the rest of her life.

After having gone through the plot, to take Sophia away from me by Martin's family, I turned to a Solicitor for advise. I explained that I had all avenues barred, in trying to get away from Martin and the situation I was in. The Solicitor advised me to divorce him, adding that Martin would have to let me go then. This I did, and it took me two years to free myself from the marriage. I was granted a house as settlement, even though I had originally stated that I did not mind taking rented accommodation. Martin could see that it was an investment, rather than a settlement, with me paying for the maintenance of the house. The settlement had so many clauses in it and life was being made intolerable at the bungalow, I felt I had to accept, what was offered. His father paid for the house, as if he were writing a cheque out, for the shopping. The deeds had Martin's name on them, how the legal profession, could call this a settlement, I do not know. Martins cousin was a solicitor, I believe this is how he may have got away, with such a settlement.

My life had become even more intolerable that I nearly suffered a breakdown and so I had to accept the house, which came with so many clauses. At least by doing this I would have peace, away from all the abusiveness, which was caused by Martin's addiction to alcohol, so I agreed to all that was put forward, just to regain my freedom.

Anne who had become a friend, was very supportive. she had helped me throughout this entire trauma that I was having with Martin.

CHAPTER 30
TRYING TO GET TO GRIPS WITH RELIGION

I tried to get back to religion and bring more of a sense of reality, into my life, by being a practicing Mormon, this proved to be almost impossible. On one occasion when Anne phoned, I was feeling particularly low, she suggested we meet at the Pentagon shopping center. Anne said that she would be meeting her friend Marion there.

I arrived on time, to meet Anne and her friend Marion, at the Pentagon shopping center. After introductions, I discovered through the conversation that took place on the very first meeting that we were all living through difficult times and had similar circumstances, with the men in our lives. My friendship with Marion, was born out of the fact, we both needed a friend and a listening ear. Over the years, Anne, Marion and I, supported each other in so many ways, we gave each other moral support and help with material needs. Also in my case I had help and prompting, from beyond the veil. As friends do, in the most difficult of times, we managed to maintain a sense of humor, whilst raising our children, throughout our many trials and tribulations. To this day, we have remained true friends, while each of us, has had the challenges with health issues to contend with. These ranged, from breakdowns, cancer and heart attacks, thankfully we have all to date, overcome these many challenges.

On one occasion, Marion found herself homeless but luckily was re homed again quickly, I went along to view the one bedroom house with her, which was on a newly built estate. The estate was lovely, and the house was spotlessly clean and modern, however as Marion was meant to move in that day, she had no furniture to move in with, Marion had walked away, from a difficult relationship. Marion and I went back to my house, we loaded my car, with emergency stand by effects. One sun bed, one garden table, and two chairs. I put together some spare bedding, spare microwave, kitchen utensils, cups, bowls, plates and I loaned Marion a portable radio, so she had some music, to help her relax. The following morning I drove round early and we had coffee and laughed and joked, about letting guests take turns, on the sun bed.

Spirit told me to go for a walk with Marion and explore the estate, so I turned to Marion and said, "get your coat, let's go explore and see what the estate is like." We had not gone far, when we came across a three seat sofa and one matching arm chair, that someone had put outside for collection. We knocked on the door and asked if we could have the furniture, the man who opened the door told us, that he delivered furniture and the old sofa and armchair would be collected, if no one had a need of it. "I deliver new furniture, that is my job, so just help yourself," he added, "I might have some nearly new furniture tomorrow, so keep your eye out, you might see something that you like He smiled and winked, Marion beamed at him, not quite believing her good luck, he went in and left us to decide.

Marion and I, walked with this furniture, piece by piece, to the one bedroom house, we laughed so much, we could hardly stand up. Once back at the house, we found that it wouldn't fit through the front door. So we decided, that the only way we were going to get this furniture into the house, was through the window so I returned to my house for some tools. Marion and I managed to take out the window. we were making each other laugh, all the time this maneuver was taking place. The furniture looked perfect in the living room, however there was only one problem. After we had pushed, shoved and maneuvered the furniture through the window, we must have disturbed an ant's nest, inside the furniture. We couldn't sit on it, as it was full of ants, the old adage, "Ants in your pants," suddenly became very appropriate. We had no choice but to take it back where we found it, so with much laughter and more pushing and shoving, we got it back outside and took it all back. All the time joking about ants in your pants and who we would have liked to invite, to sit on it.

The following day, I drove back to Marion's house and after coffee, we returned to the same house, sure enough there stood, an even better looking sofa and chair. This one was almost new, with cream washable covers but this time we checked it out, for wild life. We managed to do a repeat performance of the previous day, putting the furniture through the window, at last a home was beginning to take shape. I took the cream covers off, put them in the washing machine and dryer at home and then drove back to Marion's. When they were put back on the three piece, the covers looked brand new. The next big item needed, was a new bed but at least Marion would be able to sleep on the comfy sofa, until she was able to afford one. Marion managed to eventually buy a double bed, a few months later. Marion and I had many happy times, reminiscing this episode, that we still laugh about it today.

CHAPTER 31
MY EX HUSBAND ENCOUNTERS THE MORMON MISSIONARIES

Martin my ex husband, objected to me taking my daughter, to the Mormon Church. He took the matter up with a solicitor, saying that because I was a Mormon at the time, I was therefore a bad influence on his daughter. Letters went back and forth at the cost of hundreds of pounds, just because I wanted to take her to church with me. Martin even pursued our car to the LDS church, however we managed to get inside, with the Missionaries stepping forward and forming a shield for Sophia and I. They offered Martin a book of Mormon, which was sarcastically refused. Martin was then escorted from the church, with one Missionary holding onto one arm and another Missionary the other. They did give him a choice though, of either coming in and peacefully joining us in Prayer, or leaving. Once he was outside the church, a book of Mormon was placed in his hand, as a parting gesture.

The Church of Jesus Christ of Latter Day Saints, with the Book of Mormon giving latter day truths, answers many of today's questions, on what is relevant today. One poignant statement tells, before the end, all truths would be revealed, about people and their lives. This is coming to pass, with many famous people, taken to Court at this point in time and jailed, especially following the Jimmy Saville scandal. With today's modern surveillance, looking into the lives of many, via the Internet and other technology and medical records also being made available, many other perverts, guilty of rape and abuse are appearing in Court and imprisoned for many years, after a lifetime of concealment. The statement from the Book of Mormon regarding the tampering of foods and such terrible fighting, in so many countries throughout the world, with the wide spread of destruction therein.

It is stated, that there would be widespread decease and pestilence, could Ebola be the coming of this prophesy? Or is there yet another more sinister decease, lurking just around the corner? Hopefully Bacteria would not ultimately be the only life form, left on the earth.

This is all foretold in the Book of Mormon and no one can deny, that it is all finally coming true, for even those, who are so blind, they cannot see, cannot help, in their heart of hearts, to know and have to admit that this is true. Mankind appears to be hurtling, towards his own destruction and causing the death of so many species, including his own, throughout the world. How can such destructive acts, possible bring peace to our world, or in any way be justifiable. Peace should be our ultimate goal, not killing and murdering our own kind. We hear of those, daily severing the heads off, so called enemies and cutting young helpless children in half. How can it ever be said, it is done under the guise of religion. Anyone partaking in these vile acts, can never claim that they are in any shape or form religious. For they are in fact doing the work of great evil. Those doing so, may or may not, escape retribution here on earth, however once they return to the Spirit world, they will experience and have to endure, all the hurt and pain, they inflicted on others, whilst they went through their incarnation on the earth. There is no escaping retribution for their vile acts, once back in the Spirit world. We are the creators of lives yet to come. Each and every one of us, will have to put right the wrongs, in previous life times, this is known by many as Karma. Floods are being caused by the melting of the polar ice, this is an inescapable fact. As sea levels rise and more ice is blown up, common sense would tell us that this will only get worse not better. Lets hope that those who are involved in this, decide to put the health of the planet first. Spirit say, "The Watery Planet Earth, is held safely in their hands!" "Man can only destroy himself, not the Planet Earth." "In all things you must have destruction, before renewal." We will and this possibly now is unavoidable, experience more extreme weather conditions. I would urge everyone, to use the light, within each and everyone of us on Planet Earth, by the power of thought, surround the Earth with a healing light, so the Earth will begin the process of healing. Whilst not being at this moment in time a practicing Mormon, due to circumstances, I would have to say, that this is indeed, a true Church of God, for the truths in this book are coming to pass in this life time. Even if you don't ever read, another book in your lifetime, read for yourself this one. It is only through **love for one another and indeed for the Earth itself, can there ever be Peace and Prosperity for all of Mankind.**

CHAPTER 32

FINDING A LOST FAMILY AT RECULVER KENT

One Monday morning, after the school run with my daughter Sophia, I was prompted to take a drive, along the Kent coast. I was taking in some of the countryside, by using the back lanes from Newington school. This eventually led me, on to the coastal road toward Reculver. I felt safe on these roads, for I have always hated motorways. The day was a perfect early summers day, with warm sunshine. As I drove, my Spiritual Parents started to talk to me. "Before the day is out, you will have a Static Caravan, with beautiful views, over open countryside and a wild life park, here you will find your father's family." I had a calling as a Genealogist, at the Latter Day Saints (LDS) church, so was this just wishful thinking? No, it was definitely my Heavenly Parents speaking. How could I afford such an item? I only had £300 in my savings account. If this came to pass, it would be a place of peace and refuge, away from all the intrusiveness in life. My Heavenly Parents, knew how much I loved nature, and the beauty of the countryside. I was guided to the Reculver static caravan site, that nestled just below the Reculver twin Towers, for this was an imposing landmark. My research showed that the twin Towers, were the remains of a church, which was built in the 12th century. At one time, a Roman Saxon Shore Fort, had stood on this spot, before the construction of the Reculver church.

As I drove through the gates of the caravan site, I could see a man outside the site office, smoking a cigarette. I stopped the car, and asked if there were any affordable caravans on site for sale. He showed me where I could park the car. "Go through to the office when you have parked the car, I may have a static van, still on the books waiting to be either sold or scrapped." On entering the office, he told me, "Here we are, this one looks over the country park." He went on to explain that they had to clear the site of caravans that were too old and this one might go cheaply, because some of the caravans would need to be scrapped, unless they could sell them. He said that this particular one had the best view, the man that had bought it, had changed his mind. I asked to look at it, the static did indeed have a beautiful view and it was all that I could hope for. We went back to the office to see how much, I would be able to purchase the caravan for. The man in charge asked me, how much I would be able to afford, at such a short notice and I smiled and said £300. To my surprise and delight he accepted, so now I had a static caravan, which I had bought, outright. Also as the site rental had already been paid, there was nothing to pay until the following year. How and why my Heavenly Parents had organized this, I was about to find out. I drove home, not quite understanding why, I had been guided to this site.

On the weekend, my daughter Sophia, was staying with her aunt Helen and my son Tony, was away staying with a friend. So on the Friday, I packed a few items, some food, bedding, and curtains. I put my bike, on the back of the car and was ready to go. The evening was still bright and the day light would not disappear until late. For the first time in years, I felt free, just to relax and enjoy looking at the countryside. Once at Reculver, I dropped the items, I had packed in the car for the weekend, off at the caravan and parked the car. I then went for a 5 mile bike ride, along the coastal road, as the evening was warm and still sunny. There was a view out to sea on the left hand side, and that of the country park on the right. This was the first time, I had ever been on a bike, and as there was no traffic and it was just a straight road, it didn't take me long to get the hang of it. There was a Cafe, at the end of the 5 mile ride too, where I managed to get some refreshments. I rested for a while and then made my way back to the static caravan site. That first night, there was a beautiful sunset, I put my favorite Vivaldi music on, whilst I was busy putting up the curtains. The evening was still reasonably light, as I set about making the bed. The caravan glowed with the sunset and it was still warm from the heat of the day. It was as if my Heavenly Parents, were giving me the beautiful visual gift, of the natural beauty of nature, that I loved so much.

The following morning, I was about to discover something astonishing and understand fully, why I had been guided by my Heavenly Parents to Reculver, a place that I up until now, did not know even existed. The first morning at Reculver, I felt so refreshed, having slept soundly, due to the sea air and the freshness of the countryside. I had awoke early that first Saturday morning, to warm glorious sunshine and the sound of the birds, happily singing. I showered and dressed in light casual clothes, as it looked like being, another one of those hot sunny days. I made my way down to the cafe, to have an early breakfast. I had packed my sketchpad in the rucksack, hoping that I might be able to sketch, some of the wild birds that had woken me early with their dawn chorus, if lucky enough, I might be able to sketch, a Heron nesting.

The people on the site were friendly and the cafe, being situated on the left, as you walk outside the site gate, had already started to fill with early customers. The cafe was very popular, as you could purchase good affordable food, freshly cooked and was open until 8 p.m. seven days a week.

As there were hot showers on site, and machines to wash and dry your clothes, everything was perfect. Above the caravan site, was a lovely old Inn, The King Ethelbert Inn, which nestled just beneath, the old Reculver twin church towers. I felt totally at peace, as free as the birds, who had sung their dawn chorus, I could paint, sketch or just read my book.

After breakfast, I was about to discover why, I was really directed to this beautiful place. I went along to the site office, that first Saturday morning and asked if they had a handyman on site, who would be able to change the locks. They said that they would send someone along at 11 a.m. Sure enough, a young man arrived, who had a strong South East London, cockney accent. He knocked on the caravan door and spoke with a cigarette in his mouth, his skin was fair but weathered with freckles, which gave his skin a tanned look and he had bright blue eyes. The cigarette remained, firmly nestled in the corner of his mouth, whilst he spoke. "Are you the lady who wants the locks changed?" "Yes, would you like a cup of tea, when you have finished?" "No fanks luv, I only drinks lager." I had heard this accent and voice before, he sounded like my father. He had red hair like my father too, and this young man, even looked like a younger version of my father.

"Excuse me," I said, "I hope you don't mind me asking, where do you come from?" "You're very nosy," he replied, "Sorry, but I must ask you to just listen, If I tell you some names, would you please tell me, if you know any of them?" my father was called Chris Dodson, but he was known as Jack. Jack had several brothers, Harry being the eldest, Anton, Ben, Donald, and a sister called Betty." The young man looked at me in amazement, with a big smile on his face. He then asked me my name, to which I replied, "I'm Penny Dodson, you probably don't know me, as we have never met. "The young man took the cigarette from his mouth and laughingly said, "It's just my bloody luck." "What ever do you mean?" I asked. "I can't bloody charge you now," he said throwing his cigarette to the ground. "Why?" "Why?" because my name's Roy, and your my bloody cousin." he said laughing out loud. "You had better come along with me, to meet your aunt Betty, who is your father's sister and his sister in law, aunt May. We knew of you but were never allowed to meet you," he went on to say. "You have several cousins, Jim and Justin, Jim is my eldest brother and we have a sister too, who is called Joanne." I said, "Yes but you had a brother who has passed too." "Yes, that's right, how did you know that?" he inquired, I just smiled and said, "I must be Psychic." There was someone in Spirit form, by the name of Alex, he was standing next to Roy. Alex who had been in Spirit since a child, said that he was on the back of the lorry when Roy reversed. Alex went on to say, my older brother Roy, did not know that I was standing on the back of the lorry, when he reversed, I fell off, and was crushed. Alex went on to explain that Roy has always blamed himself for his death, that's why he became an alcoholic.

Roy's mother's static, or should I say my aunt Betty's caravan, was just two, behind the one I had just purchased, as previously mentioned, for the princely sum of £300.

As I had not held any grudge, from all those years ago, I agreed to see them. My cousin Roy introduced me, to my father's sister Betty, and his brother Vincent's wife May, I had never heard of May, or ever met her before. Roy called into his mother's caravan, "Muva, I've someone I would like you to meet." "Who, what?" I heard her shout. "I've someone I would like you to meet!" Roy repeated. "Come in" said Roy. "Muva, I bet you don't know who this lady is? I thought she was just some posh tart, offering me a cuppa tea, go on, ave a guess." My aunt Betty's beautiful red hair, was now a creamy white and her back was bent over with age. "No, who is she?" "You know who she is" Roy said. Aunt Betty then drew closer. "No, Roy, I don't know who she is." "It's uncle Chris's girl, Penny." With this my aunt looked stunned, gave me a hug, tears welling up in her eyes." Then Roy hugged me as well and I was a bit surprised and taken aback at their reactions. Betty looked at me and said, "I can see now, that you resemble Chris alright, how did you know we were here, we have been coming to this site for years." My father must have known about this beautiful place with it's stunning scenery. I told her, "I am a Medium and I was guided, just the other day to this site." This statement took her by surprise, my aunt Betty and aunt May, were so amazed at the turn of events. I excused myself and said, that as I had only just moved into the static caravan, I would come back in the morning. This was another fact that was never mentioned by my father. He would have known that his sister Betty and her family, together with all his brothers and their families, would have all had their holidays on this site, over the years. It was no wonder that my Heavenly Parents had guided me to this site, for I had very little knowledge of my father's family and my mother's family. As my (LDS) calling was as a Genealogist, I would hopefully have some information to go on.

I awoke early, the Sunday morning after meeting up, with my father's family. Everything had happened so quickly, life changes in the blink of an eye. On yet another glorious morning, looking out over the country park, I could see in the distance, the Heron making her nest. There was a great selection of wild birds here to sketch, for I was in a painter's paradise. My Heavenly Parents, had given me a beautiful setting, to carry out the work, they required of me. I introduced my two children to my aunt Betty and my cousins Roy and Jim, the following weekend. I managed to get names and dates of births, after explaining I was a Genealogist and wanted to research the family tree.

Whilst researching, I came across information, that my father was raised along with another child, who was named Christine, after my father's mother. It transpired after the birth of my father, in September 1916 that my father's mother. Christine Dodson, had a sister, by the name of Eve. I had uncovered that my grandmother Christine, father's mother, had to raise Eve's illegitimate daughter. Grandmother Christine, called the little girl after herself, to make it appear to the outside world that the little girl was her child. The little girl had red hair, as did Chris my father. Eve's daughter named by my grandmother, after herself was the illegitimate daughter of her sister Eve. Christine's husband was the father.

It would seem that my grandfather, had managed to get his wife and her sister Eve pregnant within months of each other. When I related what I had found out to my aunt Betty, she was of course upset that I had discovered this skeleton in the closet. I was able to do the work in the Temple for the illegitimate child of Eve, my grandmother, and my father in the Temple. I discovered numerous cousins that I never knew I had, I even went to see Eve's daughter in Somerset, with my friend Annie. I discovered that Eve was sent into service at 13 Swains Terrace, West Yorkshire, where she would have had to clean, something the size of the Assembly rooms in Halifax, West Yorkshire. As she was pregnant, this could not have been easy for her. Eve remained and worked as a domestic servant, until the baby was due to be born, and was then moved back to London, all this, because grandfather did not want a scandal. So it was that grandmother Christine, having a due date, to give birth to my father in September 1916, was also instructed, to take on her sister Eve's baby, once born.

Grandfather who had been the cause of this scandal, would not, have his name blemished in any way, having made his wife and her sister pregnant, within a short time of each other, it was decided that poor Eve would be placed in a Salvation Army Mother's Hospital, which was situated in Lower Clapton. In May of 1917 Eve gave birth to a little girl who was born with red hair, like my grandfather. My father and Eve's little girl who both had red hair were raised together as twins, by my grandmother Christine. It is unclear what happened to Eve, grandmother's sister, after she gave birth to the little girl. They had named Christine, after my father's mother. My grandmother wanted to give the impression that the little girl, was hers. Throughout my own childhood, I had absolutely no knowledge of my father's family. Perhaps there were, too many skeletons in the closet.

On one occasion I was asked to go to the Temple and do some work, on behalf of one of the Elders, he had discovered a female relative, born in the 1500 s. The Elder, who attended the LDS church that I was currently attending, gave me the card with the details, so that I could carry out this work. On the Saturday just before waking, I had this relative visit me, her name was Sarah, she showed me the market of 1500, where she worked. The market stalls were fascinating, some contained items such as pots and pans made from iron, some from wood. Others had items made from wool, whilst others displayed fur items. There were market stalls of all kinds, those with produce as well. Sarah showed me, the old fashioned market stall, where she worked, pressing honey comb through a wooden press. This looked very much like a larger version, of a garlic press, only with different shapes cut out to form and shape the honeycomb. Sarah said, "I am skilled in the art of Conjella." this is an ancient word, for the art of sweet making. As I looked around the market, I observed the various wooden utensil's, which were used in 1500. Sarah then asked me to tell the Elder, who was a descendent of hers, where he would find her grave. Sarah went on to say, that her son Moses was buried close by, who had died, at two years of age.

I drove to the Temple in East Grinstead and said prayers for Sarah and her son Moses. I performed the work requested of me by the Elder, I met up with the Elder, on the Sunday and related what Sarah had said, regarding her two year old son who was named Moses. Sarah wanted to be joined to him, in the holy ordinances carried out in the Temple, the Elder said that he would go to the place where Sarah was buried. The Elder came to me at a later date, saying that he had found a small gravestone with the inscription Moses, who had died aged two. He went on to say that this small grave stone along with the inscription, was found so close to Sarah, that he had almost missed it. The Elder said to me, "Do not tell anyone that you can do this." I thought it incomprehensible for someone, who prayed to Jesus, who died over two thousand years ago, and who wanted work done on behalf of the departed, should deny that they should be able to have contact, with those who would want to do this work. Those in spirit, who have contacted so many prophets, perhaps had come up against similar prejudice. I feel that I must point out, Spirit contact me, I do not contact them.

Shortly after finding my father's sister Betty and her family, my ex husband Martin, in the end, made it almost impossible, for Sophia and I, to attend the LDS church.

CHAPTER 33
MY MISPLACED FAITH IN A MEMBER OF THE MORMON CHURCH

When I did eventually marry again, it was to a member of the Mormon church, the wedding was organized by some of the members. All went well and we were joined together in the Temple. A short time after this, I realized that there was something wrong, for I received a window envelope but could not make out the name of the person who it was addressed to. The only writing that was visible, was my address, so I opened the letter. I glanced at the contents, which, whilst initially stating it was highly confidential and strictly for my husband, I felt compelled to read it. I discovered it was from a social worker, stating that my husband could only see his son, under the strictest of supervision.

Anne my close friend, who had supported me over the years, came with me to the police station. My worst fears were confirmed and that he indeed, was a schedule one child sex offender. I was told that my children and I, were in danger all the time he was under my roof, I was handed an emergency number to ring, should he try and return to the house. Social services were unaware that he had targeted a women, with a child still at school, they said whilst they were aware that he had married, they had been assured that there were no children involved whatsoever, as he had failed to inform, either the Social services, or police.

After taking an injunction out against him, I had all the locks changed and put all the clothes, that I had bought him, into suitcases and dumped them on the lawn. My friend Anne and I found it incredible, that he was allowed to attend the Temple, even though he was a proven Pedophile, we were divorced not long after.

The many strife's and tribulations, I had gone through, were enormously valuable to me later, when assisting others through their troubles, for I had an extensive grounding, in many aspects of life.

Tony was at University by now, having passed his Scholarship, to a top private school, he went on to gain a place at a London University.

Sophia spent more time with her pony and Martin's youngest sister, who was very much into horses.

CHAPTER 34
MY SISTER LETS ME DOWN AGAIN

The settlement of the house, had so many clauses to it, the house being paid for, by my ex husband's father, was effectively a loan to my ex husband. I would eventually manage to sell it and give my ex back the money, to repay his father. As mentioned, Martin had this settlement money, loaned to him, for the house, but I was obliged to keep the house in good repair and order, with Martin supposedly contributing half, which he never did. I had double glazing to pay for, plus a new kitchen and bathroom. these conditions were all loaded against me, in the settlement. Everything it would seem, was in his favor, I had to pay for the divorce, however I did not care, all I wanted was to be free of him, and his alcoholic behavior.

There were all sorts of strange happenings, whilst I was still in this house, it was built on an old village pond for one thing. Also I was seeing Spirit on a regular basis, one night my daughter could see Spirit, all around my bed.

My next door neighbor had a gentleman, who would visit her, after which he would walk through the wall and visit me. My neighbors four year old, was seeing her grandmother, who had passed on. I had never stayed in such a haunted house, it was like Piccadilly Circus, to coin a phrase, for the Spirit world.

One Sunday lunchtime after doing the dishes, I went up stairs, only to see a woman's face, hovering in front of me. It was the Gypsy, who had knocked on the door at the flat in Greenwich. The Gypsy had wanted my mother, to buy some lucky heather, when I was a child. The Gypsy hovered there for a while, smiled and then disappeared. On another occasion, I was looking after my sister's cavalier, as she was out in Spain at the time, staying with her Spanish boyfriend. I took her cavalier dog Jasper, out for a walk and on this particular afternoon, as we walked down the country lane passing Newington Manor, the cat decided to wait by the Manor for us, she would normally follow us. As Jasper and I walked on toward the fields, I could see in the distance, a man dressed, in a Royal Air Force trench coat. The man had two black Labrador dogs walking either side of him, the only thing unusual about this, is that all three were walking in mid air, about 3ft above the ground. My sister's cavalier Jasper broke free, and ran as fast as he could back to the house. Our cat was waiting at the bottom of the lane, for the cat would often follow, when I walked the dog, thank goodness she did. She ran before the little cavalier, leading the way back to our front door. They were both sitting at the front door, with the little cavalier still shaking with fear, awaiting my return, thank goodness they were both safe. My cat adored the cavalier, and always looked after him, the cat being the boss in the pecking order. During the war years. there was a building which housed those, who were in need of medical care, that were injured in battle, the rehabilitation hospital, was built next to Newington Manor. This was explained to me, by an elderly resident, who resided in the village during world war two.

It was not long after this, whilst my sister Pam was still in Spain, I returned from church one Sunday afternoon. On this particular afternoon, I had a really uneasy feeling, which I usually only have, when something profound, is due to take place. On leaving her cavalier with me to look after, as mentioned previously, Pam had gone abroad to be with her Spanish boyfriend. His name was Celino, and I was lead to believe he had a business out in Calella, near Barcelona in Spain, Celino was a Physiotherapist. On this particular afternoon, I was informed by my Spiritual Parents, to look at the list of telephone numbers, that my sister Pam had left with me. There must have been about eight numbers on this list. "Which one do I ring?" I asked, "The third one down," was the reply. I rang the third number on the list, my sister Pam answered the phone. "Pam something's wrong, what is it?" "How did you find me?" Pam had been crying. "Never mind, I will tell you later." I replied. "Celino has told me to get out, and I have only got enough money for a bottle of water, the weather is so hot here too." "Don't worry, I will get you back home by this evening," was my reply. "Where are you?" I asked her. "I'm standing by the phone in his kitchen." "Don't move from the phone, I will call you, as soon as I've arranged the ticket, I will phone you back within half an hour, with the details." I informed her.

I did not have a debit or credit card at this moment in time. My Heavenly Parents prompted me to ring my son's art teacher, I rang and he picked up the phone. "Terry, this is Penny, I need your help, I am so sorry to bother you with all this. I need to get my sister Pam, back to the UK from Spain." then I added, "Pam my sister has fallen out with her boyfriend and has to leave, but she doesn't have enough money, for the return flight." I told him, "I don't have a debit card or credit card, at this moment in time, would you be able to help me, get her back home today?" adding, "I will pay you back on Monday." Terry said, "Just leave it with me, I will call you back in minutes, with the flight details from Barcelona to Heathrow." Terry rang me within ten minutes and gave me the ticket details, he informed me that Pam needed to catch the train from Calella, to Barcelona Airport. Pam was to collect the Air tickets, from the British Airways ticket desk, in Barcelona Airport, using the number and details he had provided. Terry had very kindly done all this for me. Terry had booked my sister Pam on a business class ticket. As I had the details, I rang Pam straight away and relayed them to her. "I will pay you back on Monday," Pam promised. I changed and made my way to the petrol station in Rainham. I couldn't believe it, there was my niece Amy filling her car too, at the next pump. "Amy, your mother is in trouble, I need someone to come with me, whilst I drive to Heathrow to collect her." Amy agreed to come with me and we arrived at the airport, just in time to meet Pam. As she came through the gate of the arrivals, Pam ignored me and just spoke to Amy. Pam never even said thank you, she had been drinking on the flight back, I dropped my sister back home, with her daughter. The following Monday, all my sister Pam said, was that she wasn't able to pay me back. I had to draw all my money that I had saved for incoming bills, to pay Terry back the money, he had so kindly paid out, for the Air ticket. This wasn't the first time that I had been in trouble, through my sister's callous actions.

I found out, whilst living in Newington, that my sister Pam had given my name, over to an Advertising company. Pam had said that I was the Accountant for the Estate Agent business, she was running, All this was news to me, my two children were still in education at the time and I was a housewife, I was not an Accountant for the Estate Agent business, Pam was in charge of, the only accounts I looked after, were my own household accounts. It was only because her son Leo, had known his mother was visiting me, that the Advertising company, was given my home number. I had to threaten the Advertising agency with Court action, as they did not believe, what I was telling them.

They were demanding, an amount of one thousand pounds from me, with legal action to follow, if they didn't receive the amount, before the end of the week. So before they would believe me, I gave them the name of my Solicitor and said, that I was not prepared to argue with them. "If you don't believe me, just write to my Solicitor, and I will deal with you that way." With this statement, they accepted my word and promised that they would not contact me again.

CHAPTER 35
A TIME OF SUDDEN DEATHS

I had made friends with a lady, who leased a tarot crystal shop, on Newington high street. Lorna was dark haired and a beautiful looking women, who would do readings for people in her shop. Eventually after having a reading with Lorna, she pointed out that I was a natural Medium. I was pleased to be given this information, backing up my own beliefs that I was psychic and clairvoyant. At last some confirmation, as to what this Spiritual side of me, was all about. Lorna would send one or two of her clients, to have a reading with me, however before she did this, I invited some friends to have a cup of tea and I would do readings for them, just to get the practice, tuning into my psychic Guide.

It was one afternoon, when I suddenly got that feeling that something was about to take place, which would be very profound. I was standing in my kitchen in Newington, about to put something into the microwave, when a voice came through loud and clear, "Your sister will be taken from the Earth at this time, in order for you to do the work for her and for her to be saved." These were not my words, my

Heavenly Parents were talking to me. I felt an energy link in my soul being severed, I was so taken aback by all this, that I telephoned my best friend Anne in Rochester, I related this to her. It was just three days after getting this profound message, that I received a phone call from my niece, "auntie Penny, mum has been found dead." It was only minutes prior to my niece's phone call that morning, that a nest of tables, which were at the bottom of the stairs, had flipped over." Amy went on to say, that the nest of tables, at the bottom of the stairs at my sister's house, had flipped over that morning. I couldn't believe or take in, what I was hearing. In the next sentence, my niece was asking, "auntie Penny, would you go and identify the body? Dad doesn't feel he can and neither Leo or I, would be able to bring ourselves, to identify mum." I said "Well someone must, otherwise your mum's funeral will take longer to arrange." My niece asked again. "Will you please go and identify mum?" "Well I am very sorry to hear that your mum has passed, are you alright?" " Yes," came the reply. "Will you go to All Saints Chatham Hospital, that's where they have taken her?" "I will go and identify your mum, of course I will, I'll get back to you, after I have done this." Once more I was having to do, that which the family, should have attended to. I had to go by myself, to identify my sister Pam, I made the appointment with the mortuary to view Pam's body. I went along mid morning and a lady met me at the mortuary door, I was shown into a room where Pam was laying, I had to explain that neither Pam's children, or ex husband were available, to identify Pam. The lady told me not to be alarmed, when I viewed the body, as her arms were outstretched, this being the pose, that Pam had been found. There was nothing they could do at this time, until things had settled down. The mortuary attendant said, "Your sister must have had a hard life." I made no comment, except to have a few moments alone with Pam. I stroked Pam's head and whispered her name, in the hope that she could hear me talking to her. Pam, only a week or two previously, was very abusive, because I was not able to stand guarantor for a flat. Her words at that time, had cut through me like a knife, so much so that I felt a pain in my solar plexus. Pam had been destructive in most of her relationships, for Pam's dealings with people were always complicated. You also never knew, when she was telling the truth, in fact, I never knew the half of it. On one occasion, Pam demanded that I give her my National insurance number, when I refused, I received extreme verbal abuse, I had never heard such language, from a man let alone a woman, before in my life.

Throughout my childhood, I was constantly in trouble because of Pam. Nothing had changed, when we became adults either. Over the years people had shunned me, not only in my childhood, but as an adult too because of these lies and the pattern of lies against me, continued right up until Pam died. I had Strangers giving me black looks, who did not know me but knew my sister Pam. Those Pam had harmed, would approach me, they knew the truth too, for they were also victims of her lies.

Only three days, prior to Pam's passing my Heavenly Parents had spoken, saying, "Your sister will be taken from the Earth at this time, in order for her to be saved and for you to do the work for her.

Pam only weeks before her passing, had managed to track down our stepbrother Richard and for what purpose, I will never know. He had evidently married again, to a younger women, Richard passed away, exactly ten days after my sister. I was informed, he had been standing at a bus stop, in central London, when he had a heart attack and died at the bus stop, I had to attend both funerals, within just weeks of each other.

My nephew and niece, attended my sister's funeral, as did all her drinking associates, needless to say, her pub friends just gave me filthy looks, because of all the lies, she persistently told about me, at every opportunity. I was glad when Pam's funeral was over, I did say prayers for her, just to tell her that I had forgiven her.

Not long after Pam had died in November 95, I had a letter from Richards first wife informing of his funeral, I attended Richards funeral. There were over 200 people in attendance, for I was informed that he was a Freemason of the Eltham Lodge, Dartford. Richard would possible have attended, the Mayfield Street Masonic Centre.

Richard was buried in Eltham cemetery, he had certainly gone up the social ladder and not one of the Freemasons who attended his funeral, would have know I was his half sister, standing at the back of the church. I attended Richards, first wedding when I was a child, there too I stood at the back of the church as a stranger. Richard had married a younger women, she was my half brother's second wife. Richards only son Rupert who was much taller than my half brother approached and introduced Richards second wife to me. I had met Rupert as he and his mother had come to visit me at Newington. However all Richards wife said to me was, "You look rather pale" and added, "Richard spoke about you, and always meant to get in touch." I asked if I might have an up to date photo of him, she just said I will give you a call later, after taking a note of my phone number. Richards widow telephoned me that evening and just said that she was not prepared, to give me an up to date photo and that she would not be keeping in touch either. Richards wife just put the phone down, it's a true saying, you can choose your friends, but not your relatives.

I could not settle and was aware, after my return to my house in Newington, that I felt uneasy. When I am not able to settle, this was usually a sign that Spirit were around. I lay on my bed, as i felt exhausted with all the recent trauma. Again I could not settle, so I went into my daughter's bedroom and lay down on her bed, still feeling exhausted. I suddenly heard my half brother Richard say, "I've got one here, where's the other one?" meaning me. "I am not returning to the Spirit world yet, Richard, I've work to do, go into the light!"

As I was a Temple recommend holder, which is something you must aspire to, before you can enter a Mormon Temple, I said prayers for them, performing ordinances on their behalf, this was a way to tell them, that I had forgiven them, thereby, I hoped to save my sister Pam, and others of my family. When working in the Temple, I felt completely safe, and close to the other dimension. The Elder who I had informed, of the whereabouts of the tomb of both Sarah and her son Moses, approached me at church. The Sunday meeting had started. "I have had the work done for Moses. he is sealed to his mother Sarah, just as she requested." Sarah was a relative as previously mentioned from the 1500. The Elder then said again to me, "Don't you tell people you can do this." I thought to myself, why do people worship those who are Spirit, such as Jesus Christ and other deities. Some of these souls, have been in the Spirit world for thousands of years, how could they not acknowledge that there are many who are in the Spirit world, who still require work done on their behalf.

I once held the hands of Christ, in a sacred environment, He showed to me, the difference between time and eternity. I observed the past, present and future, also the prophets of the earth and the leaders. Spiritual knowledge is given to a soul who is humble, not a scholar, scientist, not always to religious leaders, kings or queens.

As I observed the children of the earth, I was aware that I was not in the body. I was shown my Heavenly Parents, they were very tall. My Lord Jesus Christ, explained, that they had earned their spiritual height, through their good works. Some men or women who are tall, admired or well respected, who may have abused their positions on the earth plane, when he or she returns to the spirit realm, these men or women will appear small, because their soul qualities are less, he or she would not have grown in the spiritual sense.

A small man or women, on the earth plane who's deeds were good, in that they blessed many peoples lives, and blessed the earth too. These small men and women would appear tall in the spirit world. They would have earned their soul growth by their good deeds, these though small, would have grown in spiritual stature. I was shown quite graphically, the difference between time and eternity. I firmly believe that each one of us exist in three dimensions, the past, present and the future, at the same moment in time. Also I am aware, that there are many learned people, who are in total agreement. There will be those who will scoff at the above, but I defy them to explain, how I can over the phone, talk to absolute strangers, as far away as Australia, telling them their names, age and those of their wives, sons and daughter's. Revealing to the callers other confidential details and happenings in their past, present and future. These contacts over the phone, have not just been the odd one or two but are numbered in the thousands.

I would often hear, the Devil and his deeds, mentioned a lot in the LDS church, more so than the name of Jesus Christ. Also at times more so, than that of Joseph Smith and I rarely heard the Lords prayer recited. The Mormon Church holds a lot of truths and does a great deal of good around the world, but their needs to be a lot more clarity given, from the spiritual side. All that is forecast in the Book of Mormon is coming to pass in 2014. Just as in other religions, there are many truths however, more clarity as mentioned, is now needed.

Jehovah would want people to know the truth, as would Jesus Christ, Joseph Smith and other deities. Most would agree it is time for the leaders of all the various countries, to put the health and welfare of the planet first, and all that dwells on planet earth, first and foremost. The plants, insects, minerals, and animals, these are all important and they deserve our respect. "It's a beautiful world, if only mankind would take better care of it." to quote the words, of the ending of a prayer, that a departed friend, Roger Black always used.

CHAPTER 36
SAVED ONCE MORE BY SPIRIT

It was whilst still living at Newington that I had several part time jobs, I was working in a BP garage situated between Sittingbourne and Maidstone. It was early morning and I had just taken over from the young lad, who had finished doing the night shift. He had not long gone home, when my Spiritual Parents, came through again in a voice, so loud and clear. "Get yourself to a hospital and ignore what is going on around you." Contact broke off, as a truck driver had just entered the door, after filling up before his onward journey, he had just spent over a £100. I asked him to wait for a moment, for my Heavenly Parents had asked me, to ignore what was going on around me and to ring an ambulance straightaway. I explained to the driver that I needed to ring for an ambulance for myself, explaining that I was having a mild heart attack. Looking very concerned, the driver kindly offered to stay, whilst I rang for the ambulance. The ambulance service said, that an ambulance was on its way on the A249 headed in the direction towards the BP garage, as they needed to fill up with petrol. "I will get them to stop and check you out," said the operator. The concerned truck driver did offer to stay with me but I said that there was no need, as the ambulance would be here within minutes. I telephoned Park garage in Rainham, to try and get a manager to take over from me at the garage. The manager of this garage was away on holiday, they told me not to be so stupid, and get on with it, they were not taking me seriously, so I said that if they didn't get anyone, I would have to leave the garage unlocked, as the lad I had taken over from that morning, had the keys to the garage and he was not due in until 2 p.m. and I would be at the hospital by then, I guess they must have then thought, I was serious. The ambulance arrived and filled up with petrol. The two ambulance men came into the garage to pay. They were standing there, when the mobile manager arrived and walked straight past me and just sat in the back office. He never once asked my name, or how I was feeling.

I went into the ambulance, they put a device on my finger to monitor the pulse. "We can find nothing wrong with you." One of the ambulance men stated. I had to explain that my sister had died on the 17th November 1995 and I went on to say that my half brother had died on the 27th November 1995. The date was the 15th December 1995. I was about to go with a heart attack too, if they didn't get a move on and get me to the hospital straight away. They still didn't believe what I was saying, "Please you must believe me, I need you to get me to the hospital now!" There had been just ten days, between my half brother Richards passing and my sister Pam's passing. We will take you to the Medway hospital, the one who had placed the monitor on my finger said. We will get you checked out, if it makes you feel any better. Whilst in the ambulance after explaining all this to the ambulance men, they finally decided to get me to Medway hospital, to get checked out. My blood pressure decided to plummet, they put the blue light on and got me to the resuscitation unit, at full speed. I was not outside the door of the resuscitation unit very long, when I had a full blown heart attack. It was the morning of the 15th December 1995. They rushed me through into resuscitation. I was pumped through with a large dose of heparin to disperse the blood clot, which was only millimeters away from entering the pulmonary artery. This was the exact same form of heart attack, that my half brother Richard and sister Pam had passed with.

My son Tony and daughter Sophia visited me in hospital, they were very concerned. Sophia was staying at her grandmother's bungalow and Tony was still at University. I was told that I was not expected to live beyond ten months, by two heart Consultants. I still had work to do! Why would my Heavenly Parents, warn me to get to a hospital, if this was the case. Whilst in hospital I suffered another heart attack, which again I survived. I was eventually discharged on the 24th December 1995, having been diagnosed as mentioned, with a fatal heart condition. Two blocked coronary arteries and an infarction on the heart, would deem me to be on the way out. I had strict instructions, not to lift even a kettle, and to stay in bed. Thank goodness I was given a full time carer and disability benefit. I still have to this day, 60 percent blockages at this moment in time.

The LDS arranged for the sisters, to bring my meals, as I was not allowed out of bed. In other words the hospital had sent me home to die, I was given beta blockers, which lowered my blood pressure so much, that I would pass out after taking them.

The Monday after Christmas a carer arrived, this having been arranged by the Hospital. I was greeted by, "Hi, I'm Hester," from that day, we also became friends. "So your the Mormon I have to look after." Hester explained to me that she was a Spiritualist. The Sisters of the church kept visiting and some would still bring a meal with them. One of the Sisters of the Mormon church, gave me the lectures of Ramahdan to read, which I found made a lot of sense. I sometimes use his quotes, as they have a lot of truth, which people need to know about. I lay back on my pillow after reading just a few pages, I wanted to read on but felt really exhausted. Thank God I thought, I now know the truth and it was whilst reading this literature, I suddenly realized, there was a Spirit standing near the wardrobe. He was surrounded by a beautiful golden light and he was an ancient Egyptian, the bands went across the headdress in gold and sapphire blue. The Spirit I beheld said, "Come off all your medication, just drink water for three days, and you will be healed." I felt a love that I had never experienced before, as it was felt in every cell of my body, he smiled and was gone. After following his instructions, I was healed. I was blessed with the knowledge that I was descended from Joseph, who was sold into Egypt, by way of Ephraim. I was able to walk up and down stairs, I had recovered.

Luckily for me, in 1996 Mr Thompson, offered to give me an angioplasty, he explained that I might die, the blockages were so severe. Mr Thompson got up to the third stage angioplasty balloon, when Spirit told me to tell him to stop. The surgeon said, that it was a good job, that I had told him to stop, as it would have been perilous, if he had carried on. However, he went on to say, that the work he had done, would give me another two years to live. Thanks to Mr Thompson, I have survived to write this book for you to read.

I was taken to a ward to wait as a tourniquet was to remain on for a while. Prior to going down for the operation, I was allocated a bed. My Heavenly Parents came through, unwind the buzzer from the bed head, hide it under the pillows. I have absolute faith in my Heavenly Parents, I will never query their advice, regardless of what they may say.

I was not long back in the ward, lunch was being served to the patients, as I was not allowed to move, I wondered how I was going to reach the meal, left for me at the end of the bed. I asked the nurse, if she would kindly bring the table a little nearer, so that I could reach the meal and eat it, this seemed too much of a chore for her to do, so I repeated my request and the nurse grudgingly brought the table nearer. The table was too high for me to reach the meal, so I asked if I could have it placed on my abdomen, so that I could eat it. This she did, but made me feel that I had inconvenienced her yet again. I managed to eat the meal, for I had not eaten for a good twenty four hours. Once the dish had been cleared away, a rather short nurse came in saying, "I am going to give you an injection." "What for?" I asked. "I'm not in any pain, so I don't need any injection." With this she just put the injection in my arm and I felt my heart beginning to slow down. I rang the buzzer immediately and no sooner had I done this, than five doctors were around the bed. They put a line in my arm with a drip and then tipped the end of the bed up. There was no apology or explanation given. I said that I wanted to go home, just as soon as this tourniquet is taken off. Prior to discharge, a young Doctor sat on my bed and said, "Whatever you do, don't go for any further operations, they have put, do not resuscitate, on your medical notes."

CHAPTER 37
A TIME OF DISCOVERY OF FURTHER SPIRITUAL ABILITIES

After these events, I was eventually pointed towards Rochester, to go and have a reading, with a well known Medium in the area. Hester my carer said that he was very good, and that his name was Roger Black. He was tall with white hair, and very distinguished looking. He greeted me at the top of the steps, on New Road Rochester, for he lived in New Covenant Place, Rochester. This was once a 15th Century coaching house, converted into flats. Roger Black said something rather odd. "I feel that you are someone, who is returning to me, rather than someone, that I have met for the very first time." We walked down the steps towards his flat, in New Covenant Place. I was still wondering what he had meant, by saying that he felt that, I was someone returning to him, for I had never met this man before. When he had finished the reading, I was given a tape of the reading, and after thanking him I left. He lived in this old fascinating stone built building. The steps I climbed to his flat, were worn with age, where others had trod over the centuries. The flat was not far from the Nags Head on the lower road. The 15th century coaching house, must have been a Dance School at one time, for I could see the shadows of the dancers, who would have been taught there, in the past.

That evening I attended a Clairvoyant evening, which was hosted by a lady called Norma Brown, she is a lovely lady with dark hair. Norma had a nice soft Northern accent. Whilst she was on the rostrum she looked towards me and proceeded to give me a reading.

"You are a Medium," she said, "No I'm not!" I replied. "I might be psychic, but most people are. "Oh, yes you are and I will prove it to you. Come with me to Margate this Saturday," and this I agreed to do. The Saturday soon came round and I drove to Garlinge, near Margate. Norma and her husband, who introduced himself as Bob, welcomed me warmly, we became good friends. I must admit I was feeling rather nervous, as Norma was well known and well thought of as a Medium, consequently the hall was packed. We climbed up the stairs to the rostrum. Norma introduced me as Penny. "Penny Dodson will be doing the opening prayer." This I did, "I asked for light and protection, on all that were attending, requesting that their loved ones, would be allowed to draw near, and give proof of their survival."

Having done this I sat down, Norma got up to do her clairvoyance. To my surprise she announced that she would not be doing the clairvoyance but that I would be doing the Clairvoyant evening instead. Norma then told the congregation to speak up, when I came to them. I got up from my seat, trying not to appear nervous, at Norma throwing me in at the deep end like this. I was standing there, looking at a sea of people, all hopefully expecting messages, I opened up by saying, with a huge smile on my face, "If I get nothing, I can give you nothing and you can all go and have a cup of tea early." This comment was met by roars of laughter around the hall, they thought it was just a joke, inside I was being serious. I remembered what my guide had said to me that day. "Stand up in faith, and I will never let you down," My reply being that, "I will never let you down either, if you never let me down."

I could feel that my guide was with me the very moment, I looked at a lady in the congregation, it was like doing a double take. I knew that I must give this lady, a message from her husband. I was given his name, what he did for a living, also I was given what he looked like too, his favorite meal and drink and how he had passed, he thanked his wife and told her, that he still loved her very much.

The whole clairvoyant evening, went on very much like this, I kept glancing at Norma, hoping that she would take over, as I was still extremely nervous. Norma then took over, doing the last two messages. We had great applause for the evening, from the audience. Though I should say that Norma, would have certainly deserved the applause, as she was a lovely lady and very brave to put me on the rostrum like this, being an unknown Medium.

I accompanied Norma and Bob, to several other evenings after that. I mentioned Roger Black to Norma and whilst she didn't say anything against him, I sensed that she wasn't a fan of his. I went back to Roger for another reading, I still didn't mention that I was a budding Medium.

One Friday night, I had a call from the president, of one of the Coastal Spiritualist Churches in Kent. "You don't know me, am I speaking to Penny Dodson?" "Yes, what can I do for you," I said. "I was given your number by the President of the Margate Church, Norma Brown, you have been highly recommended by her." "How can I help you?" I asked. "Well we have a Clairvoyant evening booked for Saturday and all the tickets are sold out. I would like you to do the clairvoyant evening. The Medium who was booked, has a chest infection and can't make it?" I asked politely who the medium was, she replied, "Roger Black," "Oh, mm right," I said. I was given the address and down went the phone. I was feeling so nervous yet again, so I rang Roger Black and he answered the phone, saying his phone number. "Roger, you probably don't remember me, I'm Penny, I came to you for a reading, a couple of times." Cough, splutter. "Yes," "I understand that you were due to do, a Clairvoyant evening this Saturday." "Yes that's right, I won't be going as you can hear, I'm not well enough." he replied. "I was told that all the tickets were sold out." I said, "Well, I've been asked to do it for you." I informed him. Cough, splutter. "Is this a joke?" "No, it's not a joke." I said. "You only came for two readings and you really think, you can do a Clairvoyant evening?" he asked, "Yes, but it will be packed out, as they were expecting you." with this he laughed. "So what do you want from me then?" Roger asked. "Well can you manage to get yourself well enough to accompany me, as I am so nervous." "Well I won't be able to do the Clairvoyance, as you can hear my voice is nearly gone." he croaked. I explained that I would do the Clairvoyant evening, along with my wonderful Guide, as promised. "Just come with me, to give me some moral support, if you are able to." I said in a calm manner but still feeling nervous. Roger Black said, "Well ring me tomorrow, I will let you know one way or another." he then hung up. After Roger had spoken to me, he rang the President of the Kent Coastal Church, asking if she had ever heard of a Penny Dodson on the Circuit, her reply was, "No but I understand that she comes highly recommended." "Well Penny rang me and asked me to come along, which I will if I am feeling a bit better, I won't be doing the Clairvoyance though." he informed her. The President told me of this conversation, some time later that month, that she had with Roger Black. That night I put on a crushed dark blue velvet suit. Roger had agreed to come along with me, when I rang him on the Saturday morning, so I collected him from Rochester. He was nicely dressed, in a pale blue suit, lilac shirt which he had teamed, with a pale blue tie. He looked quite a distinguished man, with his white hair and pale colors, which suited him well. Roger was very bemused, that I had only gone for a reading and was now doing his Clairvoyant evening. Me a virtual unknown, Roger could not believe it, for Roger Black, had been serving the Church's of Kent and London, for over thirty years.

We arrived at the Kent Spiritualists Church, the President of the Church welcomed Roger warmly, I was thanked for offering to step in, I felt that nervous, I was in and out of the loo so many times, trying to compose myself and asking my Guide, to make it one of the best Clairvoyant evenings ever. Roger started to joke. "Are we to hold the Clairvoyant evening in the loo then?" he asked, with a broad grin, then he joked, "Come on buttons, I am sure you'll be fine," again trying to put me at ease, whilst I was wondering, what the evening would turn out like. He managed the opening prayer and apologized, that he was not able to take the Clairvoyant evening, because of his chest infection. He introduced me by saying, "This is Buttons." I guess referring to my dark blue velvet suit. "I mean Penny Dodson, who has kindly agreed to step in for me." Once the laughter had died down, I proceeded with my Guide, to delivery one of my best Clairvoyant evenings ever. With beaming smiles from the President and Roger when I finished, I received resounding applause. "Who is she?" "Where does she come from." were some of the many questions, I could hear being asked. After the usual tea and biscuits, the Clairvoyant evening had come to it's conclusion. Several people asked me if I did private readings. I said yes, but I live quite a long way away. To some it didn't matter, they just wanted a private reading, at any cost. I was surprised, at how far people would travel, just for a reading. One weekend, there was a group of people traveling from Spain, just to have a private reading with me. I even had a telephone call at one time, from the Bahamas. The lady on the other end of the phone said, "I've got your card here, I wonder if you would do me a reading?" This was one of many phone readings, I would do for people abroad in the future.

Following the Clairvoyant evening, I had undertaken on his behalf, Roger said that he would like to go for a pint, I agreed and drove to the Golf Club in Upchurch. Roger loved to make people laugh, and whilst ordering drinks at the bar, together with burger and chips, he made the two ladies behind the bar laugh out loud. He said as I approached, that I had just done, an excellent Clairvoyant evening, at a Kent Coast Spiritualist Church, on his behalf. "Penny only came to me for a reading, a couple of times, I still can't believe it, I have been serving the Church's for over thirty years," adding, "Along comes this pint sized, little up start and puts on a brilliant performance." After dropping Roger off at Rochester, having just carried out his booking, he lent over giving me a peck on the cheek and said, "Well who would have thought it, you only recently came to me, for a reading!" Roger then started to laugh again, the scenario must have appealed to his sense of humor.

Driving back home to Newington, I was aware that for me, things had taken off so quickly. There was bound to be some jealousy, as I was an unknown Medium, who had taken every one by surprise, including myself, but at least, I now knew what I was. Some people who are aspiring Mediums, sit in what is known as a development circle, so Roger had explained to me on the way home. I asked what a circle was, he just laughed, all he would say was, "It's a round thing!" Roger went on to explain that some people, pay hundreds of pounds, trying to gain this sort of skill. I was to serve many Kent Coastal Churches, along with many others.

I explained to Roger Black, how I had traced my father's family and discovered my father's sister Betty and cousins. I went on to explain to Roger, that my cousin Roy, was the one who had come to change the locks of the caravan. To my surprise Roger, asked me to take him, for a trip one afternoon to Reculver, where I introduced Roger to my cousin Roy. Roger Black really liked my cousin, he would often ask me, to take him along to the Reculver Caravan Park. My new found cousin Roy, even loaned Roger his bike, so he could ride along the coastal road with me. With views of the sea and the countryside, Roger really enjoyed the route. Roger would always want to visit Reculver, when I was going for the day, especially if Roy was going to be around.

It was whilst sleeping in the caravan, one weekend at the Reculver site, that I had a profound dream. I was walking with Roger on the site and it was a beautiful warm summers day. In this dream we walked down a country lane, the sun was bright and the day was warm. Then there was sudden darkness and Roger was gone, what did this dream mean, for the dream itself, was very profound. I was to find out at a later date, which the reader will discover, as they read on.

The Sunday following the Clairvoyant evening, the phone never stopped ringing, I was eventually taking bookings for venues, from Kent to London and the home counties. I was booked a year in advance, after a short while, then I found that some of the Spiritualist Churches wanted to book, two years in advance and finally for three years.

I had a phone call from Roger, who asked if I would drive him to some of his venues, as he didn't drive. If the booking was in Canterbury, I would call in at the Reculver caravan site, I must say, my aunt Betty was a bit surprised, to see Roger in his clerical collar, for Roger was a Corinthian Minister.

I wasn't able to keep the static caravan, for when I divorced Eric, he wanted this as a settlement. However it had to be scrapped, after he had ownership, as he did not pay the ground rent.

Roger was very popular, he had been on the circuit, for many years. As he wanted me to drive him to some of these venues, I would agree, as I liked his style, when he interpreted his Clairvoyance, at these different venues.

Roger Black, used to walk with a limp and was in pain when walking, until one day he asked me, if I knew how to give healing. I said well it's not something, that I have really gone into, though whilst working at Tesco in Rainham one Christmas, I healed a member of staff. He had been suffering from chronic back pain, resulting in many working days lost, for him. He was pain free for the first time, in a long time after the healing. Once word got to the ears of the manager, that I was healing some of the staff, he let me have his office to do healing. Because I was able to help those in pain, I became very popular amongst the staff. The manager would ask me to do healing, on a regular basis, for a number of operatives in the store, so I found myself doing healing, instead of working as a cashier. I guess Roger must have picked up on this ability, for I had never mentioned it to him, during any of our conversations. I gave him healing and he was pain free, for the first time in years.

Roger Black had several lady friends, also a following of ladies, who would turn up at the various venues, on a regular basis. One evening, Roger who had given me my first reading, decided to visit me. The only thing was, that he left his body to visit me, Roger Black turned up in my bedroom. I had only just got into bed, when this happened, however just prior to this, I was prompted to put on, my sacred garments and robes, by my Heavenly Parents. As I lay down on my bed, a rushing wind came and with it Roger Black, who was out of body. Roger was wearing a white robe and I had to say something quickly, to stop myself from screaming. As Rogers hair was blowing forward I said, "Roger your hair is a mess." With that, a black man sat up, from out of the Spirit form of Roger. This black man, was wide eyed with surprise and fear, when he realized that I could see him. The black man had dread locks and appeared to be around twenty five, I just said, "And your hair is messy too," with this, both Roger and his guide disappeared.

The more I did in Medium ship, at different venues, the stronger my abilities became, I found myself, just linking onto the voice, of a client over the phone, that's all that was needed. I have spoken to over 10,000 people, over the phone, with these readings being performed over the years, in this country and all over the world. I found myself being able to give location, what they did for a living, how many children they had, if they had been divorced and how many marriages etc. In Medium ship readings, I was linking with generations passed. I found myself giving details, also of their location and occupations, the departed would mention, the cause of their passing.

Darren, one of my private clients, rang for his first reading one day, over a decade ago now. In his reading, from the onset, I was able to give his surname and title. I was informed by my Guide, of his families names too. As his reading progressed, others of his Spiritual family came forward, including those who would have passed in the holocaust. Being Jewish, he was amazed, that I was able to correctly name members, of his late family, who perished in the Labor camps, during the Holocaust. As stated earlier in the book, as a child in my night mares, I would be looking down into a pit, with souls who had perished in the Holocaust, giving their names and wanting to be remembered to their families, who they said, would contact me one day. I didn't know then of course, what this all meant, as I was still a child, I do know now, as a Medium.

As I progressed alongside my Guide, my readings became even more detailed. I remember doing a reading for a lady in South London and in this particular reading, I was able to give her occupation, plus where she lived, her exact address as my Guide, was relaying these details. I was informed by my Guide, that she lived near a hospital which I also named. My Guide gave other extreme detailed information, however this lady then accused me, of having a file on her. This was completely impossible, as it was a phone reading. She became hysterical, convinced that I had a dossier on her. I tried to calm her, by saying, "If you contact a psychic Medium, and this Medium is true, then you can expect to receive, such information." However she could not accept, that I could be so accurate. I found my Guide giving so much detail, height, the color of her eyes, and hair. I am still amazed to this day that I have such a wonderful Guide, he has such an ability, through the enormous dedication and service, from those in another realm. I give thanks for the help, comfort and hope that they bring, to those on the Earth plane.

I was informed on one occasion, that there was a center page write up, in Chat Magazine. The psychic line I worked for, had put the story forward to this Magazine. I didn't even know that they had sold this story, to the Chat Magazine, as I was never informed, until someone had pointed it out to me. "Diamond saves the Day." was the heading. The account being that I had managed to link in, over the phone, with my Guide and trace the diamond engagement ring, this young Bride to be had lost. As I linked with her, I could see quite clearly where it was. The young lady was due to be married on the Saturday and as it was now Friday, she was utterly distraught. "When we have finished reading, I want you to go up stairs to the bathroom, look behind the pedestal, of the hand wash basin, there you will find your diamond engagement ring." The young lady did find her ring, after we had spoken, she had then telephoned the Psychic company that I was working for. The young lady told the Customer care team, how pleased and thrilled she was, at finding her engagement ring, as she had looked everywhere for the ring. "We were able to toast Diamond, at our Wedding," the story went on to say. As I had no idea that this story, had been put in Chat Magazine, I rang the Magazine, I was informed, that they had paid £600 for the story, without even a prior mention to me, about what they were going to do. There were many other write-ups, in Woman's Magazine too. I had the news, secondhand as usual and was not informed of these either, for it would have been nice and a matter of courtesy to be informed in advance. Readers working for these companies, only get a very small amount, out these readings. It doesn't matter how many years you work, your payment out of each reading stays the same, less than 50p, you have to work a lot of hours, to make a living wage.

It was a friend Lorna, who opened the door for me, to do readings over the telephone. She had the local crystal and tarot shop and had seen advertised, in one of her Psychic magazines, an advert recruiting people, to do telephone readings, they were looking for telephone Psychics, Tarot and Mediums. Lorna gave me the telephone number, I gave them a call and passed the telephone interview and got the Job as a telephone reader. I still carried on doing the Clairvoyant evenings and Sunday services, I also did telephone psychic readings, for a company out in America, they still owe me money, along with many other UK readers. The telephone Psychic lines, involved reading for people from all walks of life, from all over the world. I was reading for many Indian people, giving their names and other details of their lives. This made me increasingly aware, how many Indian women, were undervalued, as human beings. There were numerous occasions, where women and infant girls had met their demise, with their only crime being born a girl. On one occasion during a face to face reading, with one of my private Indian clients, he wanted to know about his sister, who had died as a baby. As the reading unfolded, a beautiful young women stood by his side, her name was Pinkie and she had grown up in the Spirit world. Pinkie had been given some unclean water, as a tiny infant and had died because of this, Pinkie now watches over her brother from beyond the veil.

This particular reading, brought back the memory of the Indian lady, who had given birth to a really beautiful baby girl. This lovely young lady, who was in the same hospital ward as I, with her bed being, just opposite the one that I occupied. was crying. Her husband was very angry with her, and he made her dress in a hurry, he then roughly pushed her away from the crib. The young Indian lady followed him out, they left the baby behind, ignoring the fact that the little girl, was their beautiful Daughter.

It was stated, in the Jehovah's watchtower magazine, dated October 1st, 2014 and I quote "That in India, it is estimated that every hour, a women is killed because of a dispute over dowries. Though the custom of giving and receiving such payments was officially prohibited in 2014, more than 8,200 women, were murdered, because a groom or his family, believed his bride's dowry to be insufficient." unquote. So if these lovely baby girls do make it, to become beautiful intelligent young women, they are still at risk of being killed, just because they were born female.

My readings over the years, have verified the many truths, regarding this awful practice, in respect of the murder of female members, of the Indian society. One further example, being taken from my diaries, was when I did a one to one reading, in my home, for an Indian lady. This lady had lived with the guilt, that as a young child aged around five and was living in India, where she was born, was given the choice to be killed herself, or to kill her baby sister. She was the only one, who used to comfort the baby girl, when she cried. Her baby sister had grown up in the Spirit world, to become a very beautiful young lady and was one of God's Angels. She had forgiven her sister and said, "Tell her she is not to blame for what happened." When the world values women, then there will be peace and prosperity on the Earth. So many females have died, who would have achieved great things, which would most certainly, have benefited the Earth.

Norma was very supportive and encouraged me a lot in the early days. I owe a special thank you to her, for pointing the way forward. Bob and Norma ran their own Church too, they are a great couple that have helped many people. Whilst at Newington, I managed to gain in strength and confidence, both in working on the phone and at numerous various venues. I worked in nightclubs in the UK and abroad, Reading in Spain and Portugal to name just a few. I was also able to trace people in the UK and abroad and on one occasion, I was asked if I would find a man in Portugal, who had been untraceable, apparently for years. On being dropped off, in the center of Portugal, within ten minutes, I was able to pinpoint this person and he was found drinking coffee and reading a newspaper outside a cafe, as I had predicted. I can in no way, take any credit, for this must go to my Guide, who has never ever let me down and never will.

I was still very interested, in obtaining more knowledge, however the more I investigated various form of religion, the more contradicting and conflicting it seemed to appear, some religions do contain a lot of truths though. It's just trying to find out, which one really has it right, a case of sorting out the wheat from the chaff, so to speak. To date the last days and events, mentioned by the Church of Jesus Christ of Latter Day Saints, would appear to be spot on.

Whilst living at Newington, I did manage to help a lot of people, either through healing or Medium ship, all with the help of my Spiritual Guide. One of my neighbors came to see me, she had lost a little boy, only months after his birth. I was able to reassure her, that because he wanted to be with her, that he would be born again, but this time as a little girl, the following year, my neighbor at Newington, gave birth to a little girl.

I had two part time jobs at this time, one of which was working for a BBC Sports producer, doing various work. He was a really lovely gentleman, I gave him a message one day, as he was walking to the rail station. He stated that he was attending a Dinner that evening and I said, whilst he was having dinner, a gay would target him, he informed me that was exactly what had happened. The other message I gave him, was that he would marry again and have twins, this also came to pass and I do like the name Oliver, which is the name of one of his twin sons.

CHAPTER 38
I PERCEIVE ROGER BLACK'S WRAITH

I waited until both my children, had finished their education and University and I then made the decision, to move on. I eventually sold the house at Newington and returned the money, that Martin's father had paid for the house. Having returned the money, which was the divorce settlement, paid by my ex husbands father, I was now able to move on, beholden to no one.

It was just before, I was getting organized to move, that I had a call to help a lady, who owned a large Tudor style restaurant, in Maidston. The restaurant was dated around 1500 and was two Tudor houses joined together. The owner's daughter, was being pulled out of bed and the duvet would end up along the hall, which joined the two parts of the restaurant. I went across, to see if my Guide could help to rid this ancient property, of the unwanted Spirit, or should I say Spirits, for when I arrived, I perceived more than one, I had to work for a very long time, to cleanse the two houses. I had to say prayers in all the rooms, blessing with the help of my Guide, all the walls, ceilings and floors to cleanse this house. My Guide then gave me the words, which left the blessing before leaving, of peace and tranquility, for it is always important, to bless a house, as you leave it and to bless the new house, when you move into it.

After living in the village of Newington, I moved to Gillingham. It was late one night and there was a scratching on the patio door. I drew back the curtain and opened the door, which lead into the back garden. There was a loud purring and I looked down and there was a cat, that dashed passed me into the kitchen. It was pouring with rain outside, this little black cat was obviously in need of shelter, as she looked like she was pregnant. I put the washing basket, by the radiator for her and placed a blanket inside the basket, to make it more comfortable. Leaning down to put two bowls of food and water beside her, I wondered if this black cat had reincarnated, as she purred happily around me, I did not have the heart to put her back out in the rain, so I placed newspaper on the kitchen floor and as it was now 11 p.m. I closed the kitchen door and went up to bed. When I came down in the morning, to my surprise, there were six tiny kittens, snuggled next to their mother. The little black cat I called Tass, after the one I had lost, when I had moved to Gillingham. Tass purred happily and she was pleased to see me, Tass seemed to know, that she had given birth to her kittens, in a safe environment. I put some fresh water and milk down for her, together with a bowl of fresh chicken. When Tass had finished her food, I let her out into the garden, Tass quickly came back in, after investigating the garden. Tass was a very attentive mother and was eager to attend to her little kittens. Once the kittens were a little older, Tass brought them through one by one into the lounge and laid them at my feet. This brought back memories of the little black cat, that my first husband Keith and I had. This was the black cat, that had formed a psychic link with me, after witnessing the Spirit form of my father, as mentioned earlier, I feel that animals also reincarnate and are drawn back into the Earth plane too.

I printed some leaflets and decided to distribute them, in the hope of finding her owners. I felt that Tass had not traveled too far and that her owners would be close by. Before I did this, I took Tass along to the vets, along with the kittens in order to get them checked out. The vet gave her a vitamin injection saying, that she must have had several litters in the past. The vet suggested that the cat be neutered, I said that I would try and find her owners first. He then checked the kittens over and they were all healthy, so after the flea treatment and worming, I paid the bill and took Tass and her six kittens back home with me.

I printed some more leaflets and decided to distribute some locally, in the hope of finding her owners, what happened next was bizarre. It would seem that what was about to unfold, was Spiritually orchestrated, regarding the little black cat Tass, and her kittens, for this event was about to lead me, onto something else, closely related to me.

On a warm Saturday morning, after very heavy rain, I was prompted to go into the little public house on the corner, to drop one of these leaflets off. I approached the landlord and explained the situation regarding Tass and her six kittens. I asked, if he would kindly put one of the leaflets up, that I had printed, inquiring as to the whereabouts of her owner. A man who was seated at the bar, turned to me and said, "You must be Pam's sister, you look so much like her." I replied, "Yes, who are you?" "My name is Bill and your sister Pam, was living with me, before she died." I replied that I did not know her whereabouts, or her circumstances before she died, although I was called upon, to go and identify her, at the mortuary." Bill went on to say that he felt the house was haunted and did I know of anyone who might be able to help. "Yes," I replied. "I am a Medium, I do perform exorcisms." "No way! are you really?" he asked. I nodded affirmatively, for it would appear that the whole pattern of events, regarding my search for the owner of a stray cat, had led me to him. Bill went on to say, that Pam had died on the sofa at his house, whilst he was at his father's funeral, in London at the time. He told me that the house seems to be haunted, things move and drop on the floor, without any apparent reason. "Would you come back to the house, please?" Bill added, "I am afraid to spend much time in my house, because of this, as it's freaking me out." So I agreed to accompany Bill, back to his house, which was literally just, around the corner, from where I lived.

On arriving at Bill's house, I could feel that there was definitely a very strong Spiritual presence. I sat myself down, on the very sofa that my sister Pam, had passed away on. I could sense the fear and the panic, which had engulfed her at the time, I looked up, and standing by the television, was the Spirit form of my sister Pam. "I am not at rest, I want to say sorry for everything." I replied, "It's alright Pam, I forgive you, I will do the work for you, I want you to go into the light now and leave this house, your Guide and those who love you and mean you well, will be there to help you, Pam you must now go into the light, follow the light, I love you, and forgive you." With this, there was an immediate feeling of peace and my sister Pam went into the light. I performed a blessing on Bill's house, the house felt so peaceful after this, I said goodbye to Bill and I returned to my little house to feed Tass. If I had not allowed the little black cat in, I would never have found out, where Pam had died and I would never have been able to help her, be at peace. I was glad that I had helped Pam, by telling her to go into the light. I felt relieved that I was able to help, the Spirit form of my sister Pam, be at peace. I had been totally unaware, that she was living so close by.

The little black cat's owners, did turn up after four weeks, they thanked me for looking after her and asked if I would still take care of her, until the kittens were bigger. I agreed and said that Tass and the kittens, had been checked out at the vets, adding that the vet felt that Tass should be neutered, as her body would not withstand another pregnancy. They confirmed that Tass had in the past, given birth to several litters. I said that provided they signed a form, giving me the authority to have her neutered, I would then look after her and the kittens, following this, the owners left Tass with me. When the kittens were weaned, I had Tass neutered and after a couple of months had gone by, they called for Tass and took one of the kittens away with them, which was a pretty smoky gray kitten. I was left with the other five to re home, this I did through the Cat Protection Society. I heard that just a week after giving Tass back that she had died, Tass was left out during, the heat of the hot summer. I would have been willing, to look after this little black cat, for I felt this little black cat had returned, for the special purpose, of freeing the Spirit of my sister Pam. Tass would have returned to her own group soul and would have the freedom to roam, in the beautiful gardens, of the Spirit World.

My final place of residence, before I was to move to the North East, found me living in the flat opposite Roger Black. It was in the old fifteenth century coaching house, flat number 4. The flat shared the same front door as Roger, there were old worn stone stairs, dividing the two flats, the building being Tudor in style. Rochester had some delightful festivals, people would dress in Victorian costume, the ladies wore gray silk dresses, the gentleman wore top hats and the costume of the time. This reminded me of the time, when I had visited a shop in Greenwich as a child, the Spirits in the shop wore these costumes. The Festival was called the Dickens Festival and was held every year.

The other resident Roger Black, who I had become friends with, seemed happy to have me as a neighbor, however Spirit had planned this move, for something more profound would eventually unfold. Roger had many lady friends, so there was never a shortage of ladies, to drive him to the numerous church services or Clairvoyant evenings. They would normally collect him, from the bottom of the lane in New Covenant Place. I had invited Roger, to share an evening meal with me, as I had bought him two birthday presents, which were made by hand in Bethlehem. Two nuns had purchased these items to sell in the UK, the nuns had the items they purchased, on sale in the Medway Hospital. Whilst I was waiting to go in, to see the Heart Specialist, I was looking at these artifacts and decided to buy Roger a cross and chalice, as they were made in Bethlehem, for his birthday. Rogers birthday was only one week away in November, he was a Corinthian Minister and often did Christenings. It was just days before Rogers birthday, so I had to cover these gifts up, prior to him coming in the door and attending his invite to dinner. I covered them up just in time, with the pink newspaper they were wrapped in, which was an Arabic news paper. "Whats with the Arabic news paper and what have you got hidden underneath?" Roger asked with a big grin, as he entered the hallway, I answered don't peek it's a surprise for your birthday.

Prior to Roger arriving for an evening meal, just a few days before, something profound happened, Ian, a mutual friend of Hester, who looked after me after the heart attack, which so nearly took my life, however thanks to my Heavenly Parents warning me, I was saved and thanks to Hester too, for taking such great care of me. I digress, Ian had agreed to take me house hunting, in the North East of England and Ian and I had pulled up outside the closed iron gates, which led to the two flats. We had just passed Roger Black, waiting at the bottom of the lane for a lift, presumably, one of the many ladies who used to chauffeur him, would be picking him up. Ian and I could not believe what we were seeing, for Roger came out of the front door and after locking the front door, Roger descended the step and came toward the parked car, he then looked straight into the car window. Roger did not speak, but just stared blankly, at the pair of us. "Who is this guy?" Ian asked "For he is the guy, who we have just passed and he is still waiting on the corner for his lift. "He is my neighbor, his name is Roger Black." I replied, "Ian, we have just witnessed the impossible, a man being in two places at once, How odd, we have just passed him waiting on the corner, at the bottom of the lane, by the road, how can he possible be coming out of the front door, then be looking in on us through the car window?" I was as equally perplexed, as Ian was. I wondered, if this apparition or double was an omen. "What could it mean?" At the time, it didn't occur to me that this was serious, or that something extremely profound, was to unfold, regarding Roger Black. My research later showed and I quote, "That the Wraith, closely resembles its prototype in the flesh, even to details of dress." Also, "It is deemed possible, for people to see their own wraiths and I quote. "Among those who have been warned, of approaching closure in this case, are one of the earlier Queen Elizabeth's, Shelley, and Catherine of Russia. The latter, whom on seeing her double seated upon the throne, ordered her guards to fire upon it!"

My research of the above, and I quote, "Show that wraiths of others, may appear to one or more persons." Hence Ian and I had seen exactly the same apparition, of Roger Black. Further research showed that, "Lord Balcarees, saw the wraith of his friend Bonnie Dundee at the moment, when the latter fell at Killiecrankie," while, "Ben Jonson saw his eldest son's double, when he was in fact dying of the plague." The belief flourishes, also on the continent and in different parts of Britain. It goes under different names, such as "waff," "swarth," "task," "fye," etc. Variants for the wraiths are the Irish "fetch" and the Welsh "lledrith." In Scotland it was firmly believed, that the wraith of one about to die, might be seen wrapped in a winding-sheet. The higher the shroud reached, it was said, the nearer was the approach of death. Something analogous to wraith-seeing, comes within the scope, of modern psychical science."

The apparition is explained in various ways, as a projection of the "astral body," an emanation from the person, of its living prototype, or more scientifically perhaps, on a telepathic basis. A well-known case in point, is that of the Birkbeck Ghost, where three children witnessed the apparition of their mother, shortly before her death. This instance, which is recorded in the "Proceedings of the Psychical Research Society" is noteworthy, mainly because of the fact, that Mrs. Birkbeck was conscious, before she died, after having spent the time, with her children.

A few days after Ian and I witnessed, this strange apparition of Roger Black, he took up my invitation to dinner. Roger arrived for the evening meal, we had a laugh and a joke and enjoyed the meal together. Roger spoke about the day, that he and his brother were summoned by his mother, as she had stated that their father Anthony, was about to pass away. Roger went on to say that the Priest had been sent for, to give their father the last rights. When Roger and his brother arrived, their father had already passed. Rogers mother said, "He just drank his tea and then passed away." "Whatever did you put in the tea mother?" they asked in unison. Even relating to a difficult and serious event, Roger would always be humorous. On leaving, Roger asked me, that should he not be able, to do any bookings when unwell, would I do them on his behalf, I agreed, he then gave me a list of his bookings. That night I watch him, as he ascended the few worn stone steps to his flat, he half stumbled and took one last look at me, saying he would be alright.

The following morning, I was about to visit the North East of England, with the view to moving and settling in the North East of

England. The promptings from beyond the veil were now very strong, "I had to move North." I had seen over the years, with the use of clairvoyance, a man's face, for this man eventually, I would meet. As the years went by, so the face of this man matured, I knew his first name Jed and was told that when the time was right, I would be prompted and guided, on how to find him, for he would be the one to encourage me, to write this book and the person I was destined to marry.

I had a bad feeling about Roger, for only a few days before as mentioned, Ian and I had seen Roger Black, appearing in two places at once.

I felt unsettled, in fact I could not settle at all. This always happened before Spiritual contact, as previously mentioned. I heard Roger Black saying to me, "Go and get the landlord, go and find Maurice." I left the flat and walked up the lane, which leads upwards to New Road Rochester. There was Maurice, standing outside one of his other flats, that he was refurbishing. Maurice explained that he was rather busy, working on refurbishing a flat, "Maurice, I don't know what's wrong, but you have to investigate Rogers flat, he doesn't answer his phone and I know that there is something wrong!" "Just leave what you are doing." I insisted, "Please it's urgent." Maurice gave in and quickly walked down the lane, towards the two flats. Maurice knocked loudly, at Rogers front door, calling out his name. "Are you sure he's not out?" he asked me. "No, he's not out." I replied. Maurice used his spare key, to unlock the door to Rogers flat. The door had a security chain fitted, Maurice gave one hard push and the chain broke, we were in, I went through to Rogers bedroom, he had been dead for at least an hour.

I rang the police and tried to call his daughter, whose partner Dan had no time for Roger. The phone went to answer phone. "Pick up the phone, now, Roger has just died, I need you to pick up the phone!" On hearing this Dan picked the phone up. "I don't believe you!" he said. "I have just telephoned the police, I will get them to call you, in the mean time, I will ring his ex girlfriend Becky, as I understand she has the funeral details." Roger had given this information to me, regarding his funeral details, some time ago. "The police are on their way," I said to Dan, "Be assured, I will get the police to call on you, this is not a joke."

Maurice stayed with me, until the police arrived and took some details, the doctor arrived and said that Roger had died, from a massive heart attack in his sleep.

I rang Ian to postpone my trip North, then rang my son Tony, I told him that Roger had died in his sleep. I explained to my son that Roger was fit and well, when he left, after having an evening meal with me. "Mother whatever did you put in the meal?" Tony asked, trying to make me laugh. This sounded very much the same, as Roger and his brother had said, regarding their father's passing. Roger was only using the same humor, the night before whist having dinner. How extraordinary Tony, that's almost exactly what Roger and his brother said, when their father passed, he was only talking to me, about his father's passing last night."

Rogers ex lady friend arrived and took over and proceeded to make arrangements for the funeral. I went back to my flat which was opposite Rogers. I was in complete shock. Before midday, Rogers corpse was taken to the local undertakers, his ex girlfriend went to collect his daughter Carol and they visited Rogers flat, to go through his belongings and by the end of the day, his flat was empty. Becky his ex lady friend knocked on my door and handed me a bottle of rescue remedy. Later that afternoon, she delivered some tapes and odds and ends that belonged to me, that Roger had borrowed, she looked concerned, as I must have still looked deathly white. I lay down on my bed after she had gone and I immediately went to sleep. Whilst asleep I had a strange dream, I was stood talking to some ladies, dressed in white robes, when one came up behind me and pushed me nearly off my feet. I moved out of the way, suddenly a jug of water was placed in my hand and I threw the water in the direction of the one, who had pushed me, I then proceeded to drift towards the light. There was a loud shout, at the end of my bed from Rogers Spirit, who was standing there. "Penny! Penny! Wake up!" I came back with a start, I awoke and realized that I must have nearly died. I lay there for a while, trying to get my thoughts to focus on being positive. I decided to get on with things and rang several Presidents of the Spiritualist Church's that Roger had bookings with. I explained that he had given his list of bookings to me, requesting me to take them on, should he not be able to do these bookings. I agreed to do these bookings on his behalf, if he was unable to do them, due to illness. I explained that Roger Black, had passed with a sudden heart attack and had died in his sleep. I had no idea at the time he handed me the list, that I would have to carry out this promise, so soon.

I rang one of his other lady friends called Sonia, who was going to give Roger a lift, to one of his bookings that very evening. At first, she thought that Roger had put me up to ringing her, she did not take me seriously. I said I am very serious, she then put down the phone. I was still in shock, when his ex lady friend said, that she intended to put dead leaves on his coffin and that he would be cremated, as soon as possible. "I have no intention of informing anyone, as his daughters just wanted the cremation over and done with and there are to be no flowers." I asked, "Will you be letting people know, via the local paper?" "No," was her reply. "His family and I, don't want him remembered!"

What was all this about I wondered, they didn't want to acknowledge Roger, when he was alive either. The next day, I drove to the undertakers, where Rogers body lay. In the car, I had the cross from Bethlehem, that I had purchased for his Birthday and a wreath of cream and green poinsettias.

On the journey to the undertakers, a rushing wind, came from the back of the car, where the poinsettias lay on the back seat, even though all the windows in the car were closed. The rushing wind, must be Roger trying to tell me something. On arrival at the undertakers, I was told that the family, didn't want any flowers, or wreaths and that the coffin was to remain sealed. I kept the chalice, as there was to be no memorial to Roger, or announcement of his passing. I had his name and date of birth and passing inscribed on it. I requested that the undertaker, give the arrangement of poinsettias to someone else, or use them as decoration. I added, would you be kind enough, to place the Bethlehem cross inside the coffin, as it was to be a gift for Rogers birthday. Roger passed just three days before his birthday, he agreed to do this for me.

On my return journey home to Rochester, whilst I was driving, I must have still been in shock, for I drove passed my turning, I could not remember where I was going. I pulled into a car park and was trying desperately, to pull myself together. I could not remember who I was, or where I was supposed to be driving to, shock had done this before to me. I asked for help and guidance from my Heavenly Parents. "Please help me get myself together, Please help me find my way back home." This they did and I arrived back at the flat in Rochester. Becky, his ex lady friend, who was making arrangements for the Cremation, had left a message on the answer phone, informing me of the place, date and time, that the Cremation was to be held. The phone never stopped ringing, for Roger was very popular around the Church's with Presidents and congregations alike. His family thought that they would be, the only ones there at the Crematorium.

All the Spiritualists, Church Presidents and other Mediums turned up and the Church was packed, I had informed them that the family did not want any flowers. When his ex lady friend turned up, with his two daughters, they could not believe that Roger was so popular. The congregation sang beautifully and one of the Presidents spoke highly of him. Even mentioning how he had organized events, to support the Air Ambulance, in reality I had organized these events, I didn't care, it was something nice for him to say, about Roger. True to her word, his ex lady friend had dead leaves placed on his coffin. Everyone wondered why this was, perhaps Roger liked the autumn time, there were whispers and comments as his coffin passed.

Roger had a sense of humor, he was sat in Spirit form, on his coffin, conducting the singing. Most of the congregation were wearing black, however his ex lady friend Becky turned up, wearing bright orange, which was Rogers favorite color. There was no wake after the service, so a group of us decided to go for lunch, we made our way to the Golf Club in Upchurch. It was a cold day and we were all very pleased to be going, for a hot meal. This was Rogers favorite place to go for a pint, after performing a Clairvoyant evening, or Sunday service. It was only the week before his passing, that I had driven Roger Black to the Golf Club, for his usual tipple. Roger as always, liked to joke with the bar staff there and on that night he had asked Sue the manageress behind the bar, if he could have one of the forms advertising for staff. He answered the questions asked on the form in the following manner.

Question number 1. Sex ? instead of answering Male or Female Roger wrote, Yes please! The next question number 2. Do you mind serving men? …. Rogers answer No! I'm always serving men. Question number 3. …. Do you mind wearing a uniform? …. answer No! I find that men like me to wear a uniform, when on the job.

I related this, to those who were remembering Roger, at the Golf Club lunch, that day after we had attended Roger Blacks funeral. We all laughed as this was Rogers sense of humor, for it was nice to remember him, for his sense of humor, as well as his service to the Spirit World. I caught a glimpse of Roger out of the corner of my eye, in his Spirit form, standing at the bar.

CHAPTER 39
I PURCHASED A HOUSE WITH A RESIDENT GHOST

I was still being prompted to move to the North East of England. The Spirit World informed me, that although I was leaving family and friends behind, I would make new friends and find the husband I was destined to spend, the remainder of my life with. I was informed, he would have numerous relatives. I managed the following month, to make my way North to Barnard Castle. I had been able to get some funds together, for a deposit on a house. The one I settled on, was in a small mining village known as Cockfield, this village is in County Durham. The Indenture contained the names, of some of the Spirits that would come and go in the house that I was about to purchase. For those who may wonder, how this ancient document read and may be interested in historical documents, relating to these facts. Here it is as follows, the spelling is in old English legal jargon. A legal document of the time, with wording of the time, when it was written.

The Indenture relating to the house was dated May 1902. It read thus: By INDENTURE of this date between The Right Honourable Henry De Vere Baron Barnard (therein after called Lord Barnard) of the 1st part Edmund Charles Tennyson D'Eyncourt of Bayons Manor in the Co Lincoln Stipendiary Magistrate and Frederick William Fane of No. 1 Fleet Street in the City of London Esquire of the 2nd part & William Walker of 2 Esperley Lane Cockfield in the Co of Durham Miner (thereiinafter called the Pchser) of the 3rd part

RECITING under an Indre of Settlement thrnar called THE Settlement dated 20th Novr. 1893 and made between William Waldegrave Palmer commonly called Viscount Wolmer & Fredk George Hilton Prce of the 1st part Ld Barnard of the 2nd part & the Hon: Wm Lyonel Vane and the sd E. Chas Tennyson D' Eyncourt & F. W. FANE AS TRUSTEES OF THE 3rd part being settlement of estates known at the Raby Estates including the land and heres convd by the now abstractg presents made pursuant to a diron contained in the Will of Harry George Powlett late Duke of Cleveland deceased dated 22nd July 1891 & under order of the High Court of Justice in an Action "Barnard v. Wolmer" 1892 C. Number 2003 made on 3rd June 1892 being an Action for the admon of the trusts fo sd will relatg to sd Raby estates & under an Indenture of Reconveyance of Mortgage dated 20 Feby 1894 made between Geo. James Drummond of the 1st part Lord Barnard of the 2nd part and the sd W.L. Vane and C.T. D'Eyncourt and F.W. Fane of 3rd part being a Reconveyance of legal estate in fee simple vested in sd J.G. Drummond as Mortgage debts secured by him the land and heres convd by the now abstactg Indre stood limited to the use of Lord Barnard during his life witht impeachment of waste and divers remainders over.

In the above, I had not only purchased the said house but it came with all the Spirits of the past too, that were connected with this house. I would often pass the Ghost of some distant Soul, from the 1800s and 1900s in this house.

My research into this village known as Cockfield, showed that it would have had been linked, with a Knight called Robert de Cockfield. The village of Cockfield, also had traces of Iron Age Settlements and a Roman Fort. Cockfield village also would have had traces, of a Medieval Farmstead and there are also five traces, of possible burial mounds. The name Cockfield, derived from Robert de Cockfield, who I am lead to believe, was a Knight that had settled in the village in 1200 AD. Robert de Cockfield went on to be the one, who fortified Hall Farm.

Jeremiah Dixon, who was born in Cockfield, was another famous man. For it was Jeremiah Dixon, born in 1733 that left the area for the U.S.A. and met with Charles Mason and together, they set about surveying the disputed colonial border. This is now known as the Mason Dixon Line. This line runs along the boundaries of Pennsylvania and Maryland. Jeremiah Dixon returned to England in 1769 and resumed his work as a surveyor in Durham. Dixon was also an Astronomer and Mathematician. When Jeremiah was asked what public school he attended, he answered, I received my education at no public school. He just said his seat of learning, was a pit cabin, upon Cockfield Fell. The Dixons are the most famous local family and the descendants of the 17th century steward of Raby Castle. He was a descendant of another steward of Raby Castle, who resided in this house, which I had just purchased.

The house that I had decided to call home, was a very old stone built house and the inside was clad in oak paneling, I was obliged to have these windows preserved. So I had them placed inside triple glazing, in order to preserve them. It was originally owned by one of the Lord Barnards, at the turn of the 19th century. The current

Lord Barnard still owns Raby Castle, which is near Staindrop in County Durham, England. Raby Castle sits in 200 acres of Deer park and my research tells me that John Neville, 3rd Baron Neville de Raby, between 1367 to 1390, built the Castle which is a beautiful Medieval Castle. The current Lord Barnard is a direct descendant of the Neville's of Raby. I had not been in this house very long, which had previously been owned by Lord Barnard and then by one of his Stewards, when I was seeing the shadow of its previous owners. From the up stairs window, you could see the old Bell pits, which were mined in times gone by.

A few weeks went by and a lady, a retired school teacher, who discovered that I was a Medium, called on me and asked for a reading, I was informed that she called herself a Medium, though her abilities were questionable. I must point out that the week before she came to my door, the Spirit of a previous owner of the house, made himself known to me. He was around 5ft 4in. tall, with long white hair down to his shoulders, he had a round face, with a fair complexion. He was wearing a brown wool suit, with a matching belt, to the waist of the suit. He told me that he purchased the house in 1915 and went on to say that the upstairs window, overlooked the Colliery, which he owned, this being situated on the Fell. He also informed me that he had another house, at the other end of the village, this house was also by the edge of the Fell and said, I once lived there. He continued to say that his daughter Pat, had exchanged houses with him. I asked the Spirit gentleman his name and he said that his name was Watson Morrell. I also have a son he went on to say, called Johnny Morrell. He drives the horse and cart transporting the coal to Darlington. When I found out that the lady coming for a reading, was a retired schoolteacher and had gone to the school opposite the house, when she had been a child, I was determined to discover, if she knew of this gentleman, called Watson Morell, as I had not long moved into this house.

After giving the ex school teacher a reading, I described Watson Morell to her, but did not mention his name. Well I used to play in this house as a girl, I played with his daughter Patricia Morell, her father was the colliery owner and his son Johnny worked with him, he was one for the ladies, she went on to say. After the reading she thanked me and left. I closed the door and thought I've bought a house, with a resident ghost. I had a copy of the deeds upstairs, so I rushed up the stairs and pulled the copy from my file. There it was, Watson Morell Colliery owner, house purchased in 1915, I turned and went down stairs to feed my little dog. I was seated at the table in the kitchen when Watson appeared again. "We really must stop meeting like this, Watson!" I told him. He said that he wanted to talk to me, about the Colliery, I know you will be interested, Watson went on to say that his Colliery, was North End Colliery (Cockfield) Ltd. I was involved with this Colliery from 1910 to 1921. I only had the four men working below and just the two on the surface, in the beginning. Later though by 1921, I was able to employ ten below and four men working on the surface. This was all confirmed by my research, that which had been revealed, by Watson Morrell to me. My son Johnny enjoyed working with me in the business, he went on to say. Watson talked at length regarding his own life too. He felt unsettled at times in his life and I got the feeling, he had been sad at times, regarding some of the decisions, he had made and talked about, to me.

Not long after speaking with Watson, I went upstairs to lay on the bed in the small bedroom, when a Spirit lady appeared. She was the previous owner of the house, before I purchased it. My name is Mrs. Hammond, she addressed me, saying, "What are you doing here?" I had to explain to her that she had passed on and that she must go into the light, this lady was the mother of my next-door neighbor.

CHAPTER 40

ANOTHER OPPORTUNITY TO SERVE AS A MEDIUM AND EXORCIST

After a short while, the school teacher, I had performed the reading for, knocked on my door and asked me to take on her bookings, as she had a problem with her voice. I was asked to take on six bookings, with this lady driving me to each one of them. I completed all the bookings on her behalf. She had just pulled up outside my house, after I had completed the last booking and instead of saying thank you, she turned on me and said, "You have made my Medium ship look like crap." I thought she was joking with me at first but she was serious. I couldn't believe it, I felt angry and hurt but managed to control my feelings and just said, "Well if there is anything I can do for you in the future, just let me know, won't you?" I found out that evidently, instead of giving Clairvoyance, in her Clairvoyant bookings, she just sang or gave a talk. I had never heard of anyone doing this before, as it was the custom that apart from the initial address, you then did clairvoyance. I had several bookings after this of my own, which I enjoyed doing. However I didn't carry on with accepting bookings, because of health issues, which have taken me over eight years to overcome.

I felt the house, I now occupied was comfortable enough but I knew that I could not stay in this house, for it was fast becoming financially, not viable. I was befriended by a women in the village but found her to be increasingly needy. My little dog kept me company in this large house, along with Watson Morell. Watson would appear and my little cavalier, would chase up and down the hallway, barking at him. I was doing a phone reading and Watson played with the cavalier, whilst I was in the kitchen, doing a reading. I had to ask them to both go into the hall, or out into the yard at times, when I was busy doing these readings. It didn't bother me that I had a resident ghost, as my little dog and I enjoyed his company.

I found that people would ask me to do exorcisms. The Wesleyan religion, had been the main dominating religion in Cockfield, in past times. There were many, who were afraid to go into the light, fearful of what might await them. I was asked to see, if I could help a small boy who was having nightmares. His mother explained that he could not sleep, as every night he would wake screaming, sobbing and crying hysterically, saying a dinosaur was chasing him and he was also unable to attend school, due to lack of sleep. The little boy was becoming increasingly ill, so I agreed to go and see, if my Guide could help. The bedroom was like any little boy's bedroom and nothing out of the ordinary. Although the house was over one hundred years old, it was in good order. After talking to the boy, I asked to be alone in the room. There was a Spirit child, standing in the corner of the room and once I was alone with him, I asked the Spirit child his name. He replied, "Tom," I then asked Tom, "Why he was getting the dinosaur, to chase this little boy and make him afraid, when he was in the dream state, Tom explained that he didn't want the little boy, to be hurt in anyway. "I just like seeing the dinosaur and the little boy run," Tom said. I then asked Tom, "Why did you not go into the light Tom?" Tom replied, "When he went to church he was told, that because he was naughty, he would be going to Hell, Fire and Brimstone, not Heaven." Tom had died of a childhood illness suddenly, so I had to explain to Tom, that he would indeed be going to Heaven and that his mother and father were there, just waiting for him. I explained to Tom that the Clergy of his time, were very controlling of the people and they did this by installing fear. "Tom I want you now to tell me, if you can see a pure white light?" "Yes, I can" replied Tom. "Follow the light Tom, the light will take you to your mother and father." Tom smiled and followed the light." After Tom had passed into the light, the little boy who had endured such terrible nightmares, slept without fear and was never bothered again. Being a small village, word soon got around and I found myself, with the help of my Guide, performing other Exorcisms. At this point, I must make it clear that any readings, healing or exorcisms, are not achieved by me alone. Without the help and assistance of my Guide and the Spirit World, none of this, would or could be possible.

The following week, a young women knocked on my door and asked if I would help her, I invited her in. She explained that her house was haunted and that the Spirit would drag her out of bed and that the problem had existed, for many months. She said that she was at a loss, what to do and would I help, as she had heard that my Exorcisms had been very successful. I said I would not promise anything but would pray about it and see what my Guide and I, would be able to do, to help. I rang her the following day to make an appointment with her, to undertake the cleansing of her house, of this unwanted presence. It turned out that the Spirit of a man, who previously lived in the house, had not passed into the light, because he was afraid. This Spirit gentleman explained, that when he was alive, he would get drunk and pull his wife out of bed and abuse her. I had to explain that his wife, who had been waiting in the light, had forgiven him and the only way he could gain peace, was to join her in the light. He nodded and turned and with his head hung down in remorse, he went forward into the light. The young lady, never had any problem after that and the following week, she knocked on my door. When I opened it, she was standing there with her husband, saying both her and her husband, wanted to say thank you, for they had been about to shut the house up and move, as it had become so bad and that now, they both felt relieved that their ordeal was finally over, allowing them to remain there. The following week after this, whilst taking my little cavalier for a walk, a neighbor who lived only a few doors down, in the other direction to the young couple I had helped, stopped me. This time it turned out that it was the presence of the lady's father that was the problem. He would throw things around angrily, just as he did when he was alive, if he could not get his own way. He had objected to her getting married, for he was as controlling in death, as he was in life. I had to persuade him to go into the light, for he seemed confused at first and didn't fully understand, what had happened to him. But eventually he went into the light and the problem was solved. I stayed in Cockfield for a couple of years and even managed to organize, Clairvoyant evenings which raised funds for the village hall. Norma and Bob came all the way up from Kent, to do a Clairvoyant evening for me. It was lovely to see them both once more, we went to visit Raby Castle, the following day together and I thoroughly enjoyed having them stay. It was around this time that I had been involved with a local school, as school Governor. This involved reading through reams of papers and attending school Governor training meetings, on a Saturday, also I visited other schools for these meetings. However I had to give this point of service up, due to an impending move and also health issues. On speaking to my registered doctor, I discovered that all my old medical records, had been destroyed, so I felt like a non existent person again.

CHAPTER 41
TIME OF CHANGE

I eventually managed to sell the house, which had become too expensive for me to keep on and it was unfortunately sold at a loss. I had made some good friends, since moving to the North East, for I found it to be one of the friendliest places to live, I had ever known, also the moors and forests nearby, were beautiful. I managed to rent a small bungalow, not far from Hamsterley Forest, it was wonderful, with stunning view over open farmland. You could see the stars at night, because there was no pollution. Opposite the front of the bungalow, was a small holding, where a pig roamed free in a field, I named this sow Lizzie. When I took my little cavalier for a walk, I would take an apple or a carrot and give it to her. Lizzie soon knew, when I would take my little dog for a walk and at what time and was always waiting for me.

New baths were installed in each of these bungalows and the gentleman who called to inspect the work, had a bad right hip. I observed that he was in a lot of pain, as he came through the front door. He said that he was in constant agony, so I asked him if he believed in Spiritual healing, he said he had heard of it, but apart from that, knew nothing about it. I asked him, if he would like me to do healing on him, as I had given healing for this type of pain before, with the help of the God light and my Guide. He gratefully accepted, saying he could not put up with it, much more. Ten minutes later, he was free of any pain and for as long as I knew him, remained so. He was so pleased and amazed that he spread the news that he had been made, pain free.

The bungalow was only a short drive to the Lake District and I would do a packed lunch and take off in the car, either driving to the forest or the Lake District, I also explored the villages in the Yorkshire Dales and the Moors. The scenery is so beautiful, everywhere you go, it is also close to York, which is another great place to visit. The North East is an artist's paradise, with its chocolate box scenery and I loved seeing all the wild life. One morning, whilst I was out for a walk with my little dog Max, we had come along, what was an old railway line near Eggleston and we came across a wild doe, as we were walking along. The deer must have sensed that my little dog, was just enjoying the walk and was of no threat whatsoever, for Max just walked alongside the doe and she took no notice at all. On these walks, I felt very close to nature and the Spirit World and at peace with both. Although Woodland where we now lived, had stunning views, because it was 1,200 foot above sea level, it was very windy and had heavy snow falls, guaranteed every year.

The people were very friendly, in this village and I felt at home there, getting involved with various activities and helping out, where I could. The year 2010 was extreme, regarding weather, as most people may remember. The land was frozen, with the cars hidden under the deep snow and I was unable to walk Max. The snow was halfway up the back door and it would be over his head, if Max even attempted, to go outside. Then I suddenly got the inspiration, to dig a little trench for him. By the end of the afternoon, I had made a little maze in the back garden and I lined the floor of the maze with straw. Max now had somewhere to walk and I had managed to get some exercise too. Eventually due to health issues, I moved to another village, this time not so high up.

CHAPTER 42
I MOVE TO GAINFORD

Gainford is a really charming village, situated near the border of Yorkshire and a friend from Cockfield, Danny and his sister, plus a neighbor from Woodland called John, helped me move. I was glad to have moved to this pretty village, for the bungalow was spacious and had enough room to accommodate me, after the operation I was about to have, to undo the damage to my feet, which was due to the ill fitting shoes, I was made to wear as a child.

My daughter Sophia, came to view the bungalow with me, prior to my moving in. Two ladies, one called Louise, the other called Francis, met us and introduced themselves. They were so excited that I had come to view and they loved my little cavalier Max. The view from the kitchen window, at the back of the property, looked on to an elderly gentleman's garden, he introduced himself as Ted, he had a strong, South East London accent. We had long conversations about Greenwich and Deptford, we even discovered, that we had attended the same school, albeit decades apart, for Ted was in his ninety's. Ted confirmed many things to me, regarding Deptford and one particular street, near where he lived as a child. This street, his mother had warned him, never to go down, there were frequent child deaths, down this particular street. This address, was on one of the certificates, I have of my mothers family. My mother came from a family of sixteen, of which only six of the children, survived to adulthood.

Doreen, a friend who I had made on the rural bus, that traveled through the villages to Barnard Castle, had visited me the day before. We had gone to view the Gainford bungalow, prior to my daughter Sophia and I viewing inside. Doreen and I had glanced into an unkempt garden, which was over grown with weeds. Thinking that this was the bungalow that I was offered, we took a peek through the back window. It was piled with rubbish, to the top of the kitchen door and had flies crawling over the kitchen window. There we could see, a dirty lump of old bacon, on the window ledge. I thought how on earth, can they possibly, let property in this condition. However the actual property, I was meant to have, we discovered was close by. This garden too was over grown and full up with old pots and bowls full of stagnant water. There was a rotten sycamore and a plum tree right, up against the small bedroom window. Because of the garden near by, being so over grown with weeds, this added to the problem, with weed spreading into neighboring gardens. Rubbish overflowed in the garden and I would be obliged to sort this out too, as it was in the terms of the rental contract that I would keep the property in good order, so why therefore, was it not left tidy for me? At the backdoor, there was an old coal bunker, full of rubbish mixed with old coal, this had been used, when the bungalows had coal fires. When a lady from Barnard Castle, arrived to show Sophia and I around, it had not been painted, or decorated since the seventy's. The wallpaper still had soot clinging to it and in parts it had gone to dust. Light and wall switches hung at a dangerous angle and it cost me three hundred pounds, to get rid of the rotten trees and rubbish. This I had to do, prior to having the operation, to put my feet right, so that I could walk properly, without being in pain. I was offered nothing, towards decorating this large two bedroom property, it was a case of, accept it or go right back, to the bottom of the list, for Association property.

There are many residents in the UK, who end up making good, property which should be the responsibility, of the Landlords, in this case the Housing Association. However as I had a badly infected foot at the time, due to a botched operation and as I had to use a wheelchair, I was grateful to move into a wheel chair, friendly property.

The operation had been performed with an epidural, in one of the oldest operating theaters in Darlington hospital, with no anesthetist present, or theater nurse in attendance. There was just the Indian orthopedic surgeon and his unqualified assistant present. The surgeon asked me, when I was on the table in theater, if I minded someone unqualified being there, I thought he was joking but he wasn't. The theater did not have a sterile air flow. A ward nurse, who I recognized from the ward I was on, prior to being taken down, to the theater for surgery, walked in on the operation, in clothes which were far from being clean and definitely not sterile. He called to the surgeon, who was in the middle of operating. "Shall I take her away now." "Not now, Vinnie," shouted the Indian surgeon, adding, "Get out! Vinnie." This was the same male nurse, who had been pushing a thermometer into my ear, without the ear guard, in place. There was no cover, to stop me looking, at what was going on during the operation and I could see on the monitor that the surgeon, had severed the ligament to my large toe on my left foot. On leaving the hospital, I had infection under the theater bandages, due to the lack of care shown during this operation, by this Indian surgeon.

I went home by taxi and hobbled into the bungalow, thank goodness I had my desk chair that had wheels, near the front door. I was able to get around on this, until Doreen bless her, manged to get the loan of a wheel chair for me. I was in such pain with this foot and had to call the district Nurses in to dress the foot everyday. The foot was so badly infected, under the theater bandages that it took nine weeks, before the infection was under control. My toe, which had the ligaments severed, was hanging away from the foot and I had to put blue support bandages on everyday, so that the toe had some kind of support.

The foot was eventually put right, by a brilliant young surgeon, who also proceeded to put the other toes right. All the reconstructive operations this time, were performed with anesthetists and theater nurses being there. The operating theater was clean and sterile and my sincere thanks, go to this brilliant young English surgeon.

I made friends with a lady called Jane, who offered to look after Max, my little cavalier, whilst I was under going various operations, one also being to give me my sight back. I had to have lens transplants, in both eyes due to cataracts. This again was an operation, which wasn't to go well, as the surgeon who was performing the operation on the right eye, bumped his head on the equipment. He bled profusely all over the lens, just as he was about to put the new lens in, meaning the lens was unable to be used, with another surgeon being called in, to finish the operation. "Is there a Doctor in the house?" one of the attending nurses laughingly asked. The next sentence to the ophthalmic surgeon, from the nurse was, "You can't put that lens in, it has a defect and is not suitable." However I am grateful that he saved the day and my sight, as my own lens at this time had been removed. Although the lens had a defect, he said, "That will do splendidly," putting the defective lens in the eye, instead of the perfect one that should have been used. So ultimately, although he saved my sight, there was one drawback, in that I have a permanent coma defect, on the lens, which makes it difficult to read figures and also gives me poor vision in my right eye. As I am a writer and an artist, this makes life more difficult, so perhaps the reader will allow, for any **misplaced commas** contained within this book. Well that's my excuse and I'm sticking to it, I state this tongue in cheek and not as a definite fact.

I am sure I'm not the only victim, of these sort of Medical mishaps and I subsequently managed to get an appointment, with another ophthalmic surgeon, who was due to retire. He talked me out, of having any further surgery on the eye, that had the defective lens in, saying it was too hazardous and it would be better, to just buy a pair of distance glasses, he went on to say that he was the one, who had trained the surgeon, who had put the defective lens in my right eye. Whether this was a misplaced boast, or a statement of failure, I don't know. I was dismayed to read at a later date, that he had put on the form, that I had refused treatment, when in actual fact I had not. I would have been so pleased, if they had rectified the situation, by replacing the defective lens. In life, the Spirit World gives us all sorts of challenges. Some in the pre - existence, choose other forms of challenges, before they come into existence, in the Earth Plane.

If you are a Medium reading this book, I am sure that the Spirit World, would have given you too, a great deal of challenges, to strengthen your Medium ship.

CHAPTER 43
THE EVENT MENTIONED BY SPIRIT CAME TRUE

Shortly after I moved to the beautiful village of Gainford. My little cavalier Max passed, with a leaky heart valve and I felt completely alone at this point in time, not able to get out and about, because of health issues, I sat in the front room, feeling desperately alone and then came a voice from my Heavenly Parents, "The one we have shown you clairvoyantly, all your life, is waiting for you."

They gave me his email address saying, "You will recognize him still, even though he is now retired." I had seen at various times in my life clairvoyantly and in dreams, a man who I felt I knew, but was yet to meet. The reader may doubt, that Spirit could possibly, give me the email address of someone. However, if the reader would take a moment to reflect and think about this, how would my Guide, be able to give me the names, locations, age, married or otherwise and their occupations in life, of all those I had given readings for? Also, to be able to give, other private and intimate details of people of all nationalities, who I have never even met, both in the UK and various parts of the globe. Obviously, I would have no time whatsoever, to do any research on my clients, so how am I able to do so? The answer is quite simple, my Spiritual Guide Joseph, relays all this to me, at the time in question. There is no way, could I have a dossier on everyone, in all parts of the World, but my Spiritual Guide has. Guessing would be out of the question, in all these cases, as the chances of always being right and accurate is infinitesimal and I would so easily be proven, to be a charlatan.

I complied and did as I was instructed, and I found my future husband, the one I had seen at various times in my life, over the years Clairvoyantly. We corresponded for a while and we were engaged and married the following year in 2013. To this day I am extremely happy, as we have a lot in common, for Jed is very psychic and a man in every sense of the word. He is able to tell me, exactly what I am thinking, even before I have time to say it.

Jed and I were on a train, heading back up North, after a visit to London. We were sitting opposite a couple, when the strangest thing happened. I suddenly could see Keith my first husband, who had passed years ago with cancer. Keith had a man standing next to him, who had passed, Keith introduced this man, who informed me, that he was the father, of the lady seated directly opposite. Keith said that they were both in the Royal Marines, in the same boat, when rescued from their ship, after it was sunk by a torpedo. The lady's father, then asked me to tell his daughter, what he looked like and this I did, describing his height, the color of his hair and that of his eyes. The lady sat wide eyed and utterly dumb founded. Her father then said, "Tell her, she has a photograph of me, in her purse," her father said. When I related this to her, she declared adamantly, "No I don't have a photo of him, sorry." "Insist that my daughter looks inside her purse," knowing that Spirit never lie, I therefore asked her, to look inside her purse. This she did and to her great surprise, there was the photo of her father, for she had forgotten that this photo, was even in her purse. "Tell her that I am pleased that she is getting married again, I will be there in Spirit." With that, the impromptu reading ended. My first husband Keith, was the other survivor in the life boat, with her father, they were in the Royal Marines together.

Having performed many Clairvoyant evenings and over 10,000 readings, on the telephone alone, the above events, also convinced me, to write this account, of my Fight back to Eternity.

I have been prompted to add, that on Christmas Eve 2014 there will be, yet another extreme weather event, to do with flooding, so perhaps we all should be prepared. It would be nice, if funds could be put aside for those in need, being made available in the UK, to prevent further flooding, before millions of pounds, are sent elsewhere. I feel it should be our duty, to care for our own and others who are in the UK, with this being our main priority. The public will need the Army in the coming years, so all those brave souls, who have served abroad, hopefully will not be made redundant, on their return. They have faithfully served us as a country and they have put their lives on the line, to try and make this world a better place, for all who live in it. Many of those in power and high places, must put the welfare of the Planet as a whole first, before it is too late, using the resources, to benefit the whole of mankind and the animal kingdom, not just the privileged few.

Spirit say, that the planet Earth, or the Watery planet, as she is know by Spirit, is in their hands. The Earth will and does cleanse herself, whilst still being held, in the safe hands of the Spirit World. This was repeated by my Heavenly Parents, that the Earth will be safe and always will be, for those in the Spirit World will safely guard it, for the Earth is used, for the perfection of the soul qualities.

My research shows and I quote that "The large Hadron Colider, that was subscribed to, by all the Banks around the world, is the highest-energy particle Colider ever made, which started up, on the 10th September in 2008." But I understand whilst researching this, that as a practical tool, it's no match for the UK's *Diamond* Light, now there's a coincidence. I heard from a quote, that Professor Stephen Hawkins adds a proviso, that there is a risk involved, that these experiments could cause the Earth to implode and it would take a brave man to dispute him. But I still feel that the watery planet, is held safe in the hands of the Spirit World. I feel that the answers can also be gained, as we link to the Spirit World. We are all Spiritual beings and at the end of time, it is to the Spirit realms, that we must all return, before we can explore the universe and solve the question of existence. Quarks which are two up and two down, make the building blocks of life, in the world of matter. These facts that have been discovered by Science, could have been given by the Spirit World, without all the expense, of such large complicated machinery.

The Etheric Double of the body interpenetrates. This is why, when someone has a limb amputated, they still feel that they have that limb, attached to their body. The aura surrounds them and can be seen with practice, if you hold your hand, against a *plane* background, you can eventually see the aura and the colors, however this takes practice. The etheric body vibrates at a different level, as the etheric is composed of a lighter physical matter. There is also super etheric, sub-atomic and atomic, these can all be seen clairvoyantly. I looked inside a flower with my clairvoyant vision and it is beautiful, this light that emanates within the flower, has the gold of creation.

The physical body is also supplied energy, via the Chakra's, these are the energy centers within the body. In this way the physical body is supplied with vitality, necessary for its existence and its well being during life.

The etheric double links, the physical and the astral bodies, for without it, there could be no communication, with the astral world, neither thoughts or feelings. As mentioned, anesthetics push out the etheric double, and make the patient free of pain. In dreams the etheric part of the brain is extremely active and some clairvoyants receive information in this way. Shortly after death, the Etheric double leaves the physical body, though it does not at first, move far away from that body.

I once observed President Clinton, sat in a Bay window, which overlooked the lawns, in the White House and before the reader inquires, No! Monica Lewensky, was not present at that moment in time. In his hand he held some papers, which were pale green in color and several men in dark business suits, entered the large paneled door, to his office. And so it is, if you are an evolved soul, you may travel and look into events, not only in the lives of the people, in this present life time, but also look into the lives of those past. The Earth, being a heavier form of matter, is like the layers of an onion. One layer of time and then another layer of time, so it is in Spirit. In the Spirit World, you can look back in time and forward in time, for time has no beginning and no end. As Governments turn on their own people and weather patterns change, many Souls will return to the Spirit World. For decades evil leaders, have used the common man, woman and child. Lives have been sacrificed, at the whim of these leaders. Nature and the Animal kingdom, all sacrificed for their own gain. Some Corporate companies, it has now been disclosed by Scientists, have put substances which have added toxins, not only in packaging but in the foods and drinks too. These I believe, have gone on to cause Cancer and Heart decease in the populous of the Earth. Age discrimination, now has been put forward, regarding Medical treatment. There is now a statement out that those over the age of sixty five, or of no further use to society, may not receive the Medical treatment, which would save their lives. NICE have been instructed by the Government, that they should only allow those, who are considered to be of any further use to society, to be given the latest drugs, which could and would save their lives. This was also quoted, in The Express News Paper, 19th February 2014 which went on to say, that the House of Commons was in uproar, regarding this latest piece of legislation. The Government have already displaced thousands and whole families have had their lives, turned upside down, due to the legislation passed in 2013, the dreaded *Bedroom Tax*. Thought has apparently been given, to follow Darwin's natural selection theory of 1859. This could possible include, newly born with defects, not being given a fighting chance of survival, hopefully this is just a plan and nothing more.

We have already witnessed, the malpractice of hospitals towards patients. I have personally witnessed, a women being admitted with a broken leg and given nothing to eat or drink, from the Monday to the Friday, when she died. There was no saline drip in place either, she was only given Diamorphine, also known as Heroin, this lady never regained consciousness. Another patient, was left standing at a sink for over an hour. I placed a bowl under her, because she was pleading with the nursing staff, to help and take her to the toilet.

Evil Governments around the world, are turning on their own people, as forecast in the Holy Scriptures, Father against Son, Neighbor against Neighbor.

The weather patterns have changed, again prophesied in the Holy Scriptures. All the above is written in scripture and I truly believe that all will come to pass.

At the end of each Soul's life, they must undergo a life review. Those Souls who have made others suffer, will in turn feel every hurt, and fear that they have inflicted on others. We are all judged by our Soul qualities, every deed good or bad is noted. Every work good or bad is noted and every word spoken is recorded. Life will be shown like subtitles, with all the accompanying feelings, good or bad, that have been felt by their beneficiaries or victims. Having had, more than one near death experience, I know this to be true.

If you choose to reincarnate, I believe, that you will be given the chance to put right, some of these wrongs, depending on the Soul who is willing to do just that. There are many references to this school of thought in religious literature too. We can either choose to take on board these truths, or ignore them. It is our choice, as we are all Souls incarnate, having an Earthly experience. My Heavenly Parents inform me, that we are all part of the Spirit World and that first and foremost we must not forget that each and everyone of us are Spirit, we are indeed in the hands of the Spiritual realm. As we are part of the watery planet, so it is our bodies are water too.

Your hands, can create beauty or ugliness. You can bless or destroy but each event is creative, because of the laws of cause and effect. Those who live and choose to enhance their lives and the lives of others, are well on their way to perfection. All life reviews are listed in the Akashic records of life. If the Etheric or Soul body wishes another Earthly life, they know the challenges which they will undertake.

There are many who have lived on Earth before, sometimes as male and other times as female. Some souls return, to put right the wrongs they have perpetrated, in a previous life, or to teach Spiritual truth and knowledge.

If a man strikes a match and burns down the forest, he has set in motion a multitude of events. He has destroyed the plants that heal and give life. He has destroyed the habitat of the animals and insects, which play an equally important role in nature. He has destroyed the habitat of the humans that rely on all the above for life. He has started a chain of destruction, of the very air it's self, for all is cause and effect.

Planet Earth is a living entity. Even a crystal is a form of life, the ancient Egyptians would at times, use a crystal to heal. As we go through our own incarnation, give a thought to Planet Earth, which is your home and use your time on Earth wisely. Bless the Earth, with your presence so she may in turn, Bless you, and those that come after you.

CHAPTER 44
IN A SACRED MEETING I WAS SHOWN THE PAST, PRESENT AND FUTURE

I was shown the past, present and future during a sacred blessing, as stated earlier in this book. I had fasted for three days before undertaking this blessing. As the Patriarch placed his hands above my head, I could feel movement, as if a butterfly gently fluttered above my hair. As the blessing unfolded, I was aware of a bright light. I could see the Christ figure, sat on a white rock, the light was the purest of white light and not like any, I had ever seen on earth.

I was aware that I was no longer in my earthly body, I was instructed to hold the hand of Christ. Christ said to me, "I am going to show you, that which has frightened you all your life, the difference between time and eternity." As I looked, I could see that the past, present and future were all existing together. You could travel back to the past, see the present and go forward to a time of the future. I had time and eternity relating to the earth plane, shown before me. I had this, graphically shown to me that past, present and future exists together. One of the profound sights, were of when the enslaved tribes fled Egypt and the waters parted, to enable them to reach safety, the waters then closed over the Army of Pharaoh, I always thought this was a fairy tale.

Christ spoke to me again, saying that I would remember at times, when needed, the information that had been shown to me, I had also been shown my Heavenly Parents, who were very tall Spirits.

When the Soul wishes to incarnate, it first comes through the Ether and forms the Etheric body, which is a lighter form of matter. The oval light of the Soul, hovers near the aura of the chosen mother. It enters the oval shape of the egg, at the moment of conception, there to form the mortal cloak, which is made up of all the elements, of this particular planet. I am firmly convinced, from what I had been shown, that the mortal soul undertakes several incarnations, before it reaches perfection. The casual body, is when the soul has reached perfection, in that it is the body eternal. All of the bodies, which the soul interpenetrates are interwoven. Such as the Astral, Etheric, Mental bodies and the ego. These bodies differ, in that they are vibrating at different levels. So they vary in density, depending on the matter they are composed of but they interpenetrate each other. There is an atomic and a sub atomic level as previously mentioned. The final body, has been fully developed, once the Soul has gained the full knowledge of the Spiritual, through its various incarnations. The bottom line, is that you are Spirit here and now, having an earthly experience, in order that you might grow Spiritually and gain truth and knowledge in all things, thus understanding things, as they really are. You don't die, you may rest for a while in the realm, you will then go on, until you have manged, through various incarnations, to attain perfection.

Planets are not just, our home, they are living energy and so are we, for we are part and parcel of this living energy, made up of all the same materials. As previously mentioned, energy cannot be destroyed, the forces that are energy, are both positive and negative, neutrons and protons, atoms and particles, atomic, sub atomic. All these are part of the living structure of the planet, we all are part of this mix, of living structure of the planet. Planet earth is mainly water, so if think about it, we are too.

If we live negatively, a planet will implode sooner, rather than later. Positive and creative thought, together with positive deeds, holds the planet in balance and in harmony. The same applies to our mortal cloak, our bodies.

The negative is destruction and decease, hence the dark verses the light. Creative positive mind energy, does the opposite, we label this energy the God force, as positive energy creativeness, brings what we label as miracles, Spiritual knowledge.

Negative and Positive is found in all life, animal, vegetable and mineral. Animals can either be of a good nature, or a dangerous nature. Plants can heal and cure, they can sustain us, but they can also kill us. This also is true with a virus, which can either be good or bad.

As evolved people, tap into this positive energy with their minds, they have the powers to heal and renew, using this positive life force. Everything has its opposite, these forces are labeled, in order for us to try and comprehend, the various forms of energy. Some use, what I would call dark energy, which is negative and destructive. Humans have understood these energies, by calling them by various names, be it scientific names, or religious names.

Our own energy, is creative or destructive, everything has an opposite, all in some way are creative. Your mind energy can bless and heal, or be destructive. We all know that the way we live our lives and use our mind energy, helps us evolve.

As we incarnate, the physical, which is the heavier form of matter, we learn through positive and negative forces, to reach perfection and gain understanding, of all the creative side of our existence.

So use your mind energy in a positive way, to send out a protective light around the world. You can not have darkness, where there is light, we are all part of the same energy. You cannot destroy energy, you simply become a lighter form of matter, once you are no longer part of the mortal cloak, which is a heavier form of matter, eventually you become a body of light.

Our energy is both male and female, for all baby's have this male and female element within them. Some species though male, can change to female and procreate. Female energy by nature is more creative, whilst Male by nature, has more of the destructive elements. So value the positive elements of female energies, for they are also within the male energy too. **Put away your fear of death, you cannot destroy the energy which you are made up of.** Our Planet Earth was born of a star, our Sun, we are part of that star. We have the element of the Sun within us too, some times the energy of the Sun within us, over takes our bodies, the body can then, self combust.

At the end of a planets life, negative energy is disposed of, in the fire of the Earth. Hence the label, hell, fire and brimstone. This is where all the negative energy is sucked into, at the end of the last days of the planet's life. So choose wisely as you take this incarnation, between positive and negative. Value the positive energy and you will evolve to perfection, the planet will also benefit as you will too.

Some evolved positive energies, will go on to form other planets, for these are creative energies, which construct other worlds. Death of the Mortal Cloak, is only the beginning of the next stage of life.

Have no fear of death, for dying is not the end, merely a new beginning, for the release of the mortal cloak, gives us the opportunity, to go forward and fulfill our future destinies.

Alpha and Omega

Diamond Alpha Omega
Diamond is a World Famous Psychic Medium, healer and Exorcist who has helped many people in all walks of life with her gifts; working over the telephone reaching out to tens of thousands or more giving help and guidance to bring comfort and reassurance. Diamond has been mentioned in various publications and Magazines working in public on stage and platform in a caring sensitive way reaching out to many.
A genuinely gifted lady.

Made in the USA
Charleston, SC
28 July 2015